The Saxophone, How It Works

The Saxophone, How It Works

A Practical Guide to Saxophone Ownership

Michael J. Pagliaro

Co-Published in Partnership with the
National Association for Music Education

ROWMAN & LITTLEFIELD
Lanham • Boulder • New York • London

Published by Rowman & Littlefield
An imprint of The Rowman & Littlefield Publishing Group, Inc.
4501 Forbes Boulevard, Suite 200, Lanham, Maryland 20706
www.rowman.com

86-90 Paul Street, London EC2A 4NE

Copyright © 2024 by The Rowman & Littlefield Publishing Group, Inc.

All rights reserved. No part of this book may be reproduced in any form or by any electronic or mechanical means, including information storage and retrieval systems, without written permission from the publisher, except by a reviewer who may quote passages in a review.

British Library Cataloguing in Publication Information Available

Library of Congress Cataloging-in-Publication Data

ISBN: 978-1-5381-9078-4 (pbk)
ISBN: 978-1-5381-9079-1 (ebook)

Table of Contents

Acknowledgments vi

Introduction vii

1. What Are the Parts of My Saxophone? 1

2. How Does My Saxophone Work? 5

3. What Are the Different Kinds of Saxophones? 17

4. How Are Saxophones Made? 23

5. How Do I Take Care of My Saxophone? 31

6. How Should I Plan My Practice Sessions? 39

7. A Survey of the History of Woodwind Instruments 43

8. What Items (Accessories) Will I Need to Help Me Play My Saxophone? 65

Appendix 81

The Science of Sound 81
Glossary of Woodwind Instrument Terms 87
Dictionary of Saxophone Terms 93
Index of Saxophone Parts 97
Saxophone Mouthpiece Design 99
Instrument Ownership Record 102

Index 107

Acknowledgments

The following extraordinarily gifted musical instrument fabrication and distribution professionals have generously granted permission to use information and artwork from their websites. Listed in alphabetical order, they are:

Donna Altieri Bags, info@altieribags.com

Erick D. Brand, for permission to show the clarinet key system diagram from the Erick D. Brand Band Instrument Repair Manual

How It's Made, https://www.sciencechannel.com/show/how-its-made-flute

Lars Kirmser, publisher and musical instrument specialist at http://www.musictrader.com

Julius Keilwerth, for permission to use pictures from, his website. https://www.julius-keilwerth.com/en/

Theo Wanne, author of Saxophone Mouthpiece Design for permission to use that information in the appendix. http://TheoWanne.com

Rick Wilson, for permission to use his Historical Flute Page at http://www.oldflutes.com/boehm.htm

Introduction

The method book you are now using was written to help you learn how to play the Saxophone. That book contains information on holding your saxophone, making a sound, reading music, playing different notes, and much more.

This book will teach you additional information about your instrument to help you better understand how it works, how to work it, care for it, and how to be a more knowledgeable saxophonist.

The first section of this book reviews information that might be on the first few pages of your method book. Even if you know that information, spend a few moments reading this section to see if you can find something you have not yet learned. You will be learning information about the saxophone that not many students will ever know.

You do not have to read this book in the order in which the chapters appear. Start at any chapter that interests you, and then, as you progress, move to the chapters related to your saxophone studies. Because you can read any chapter, some needed information is repeated to cover the issue under study.

NOTE: In music, the term head joint can also be written as one word. You might see it as headjoint.

Chapter 1

What Are the Parts of My Saxophone?

The Instrument—The saxophone is made of brass and uses a single reed mouthpiece. The instrument is made in three sections. The mouthpiece (A), neck (B), and body (C).

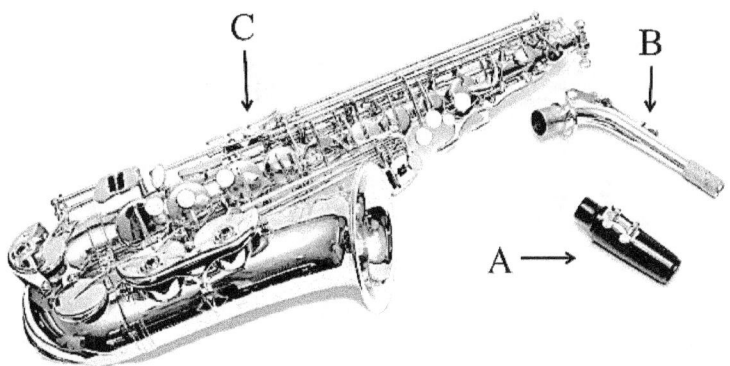

Saxophone Parts

Below is a picture of a saxophone with its parts labeled. Take out your saxophone and locate the labeled parts on your instrument.

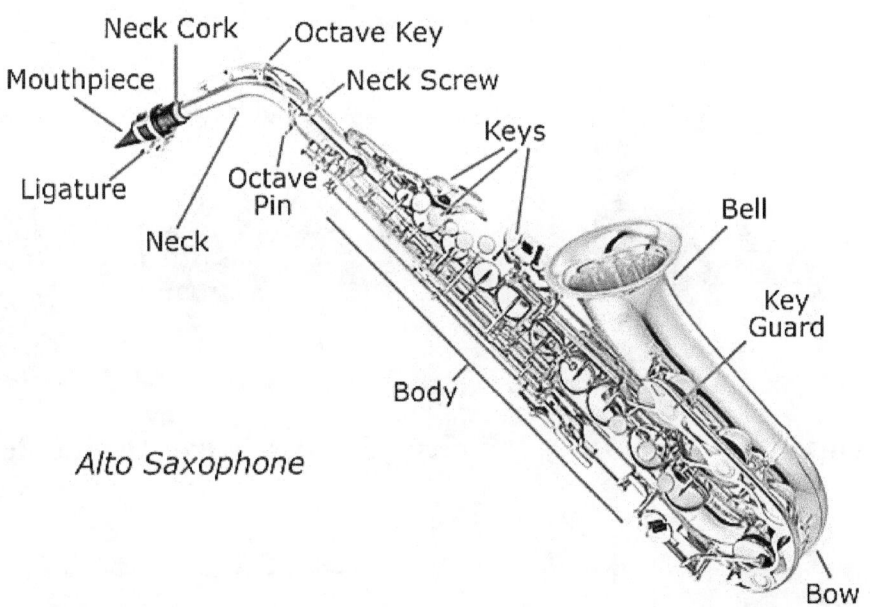

(http://www.bing.com/images/search, 2014) *"Free to share and use commercially."*

A closeup shows how the neck (A) is placed into the body (B), being careful not to bend the octave key (C).

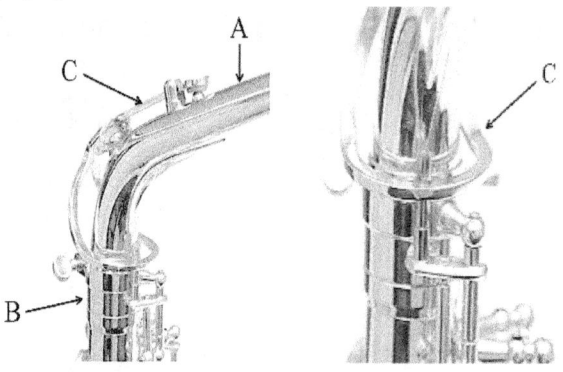

Detailed Saxophone Parts

This section is repeated in the appendix with page numbers for easy reference.

Bell **Body** 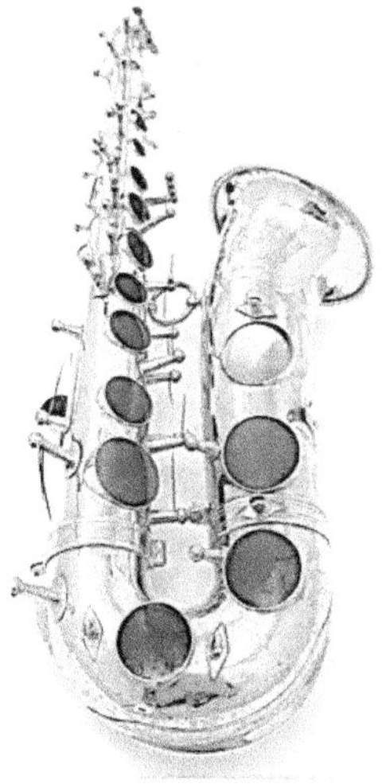 **Bridge (octave, pin) Key**

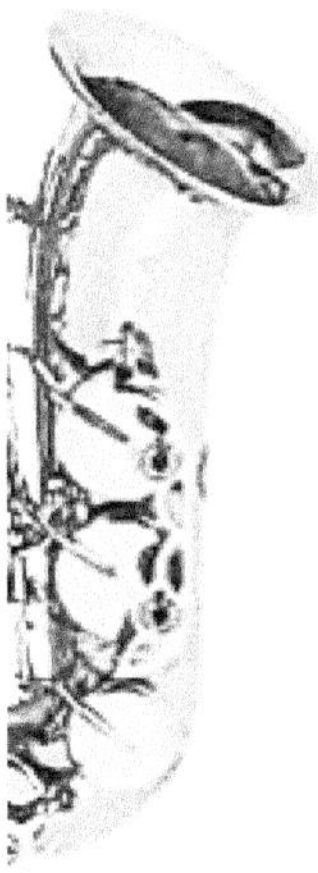

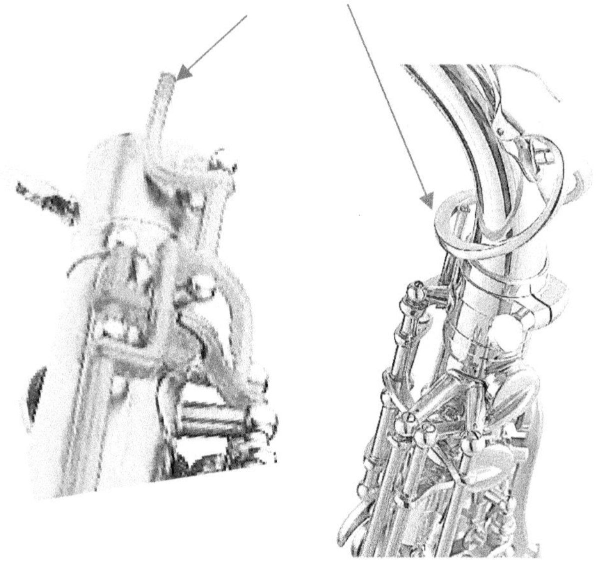

Pad cup 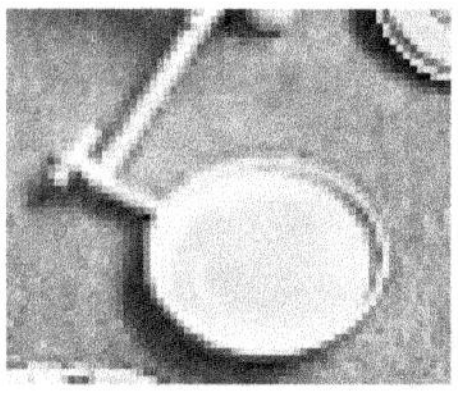 **Key Springs, wire, needle, flat**

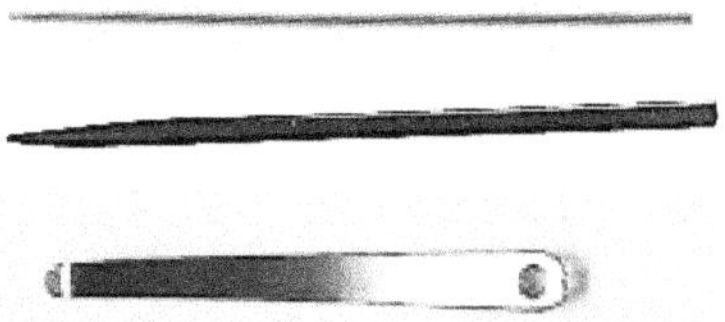

Ligature	Mouthpiece	Key System
		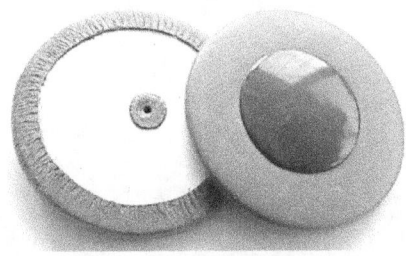

Neck	Octave Key	
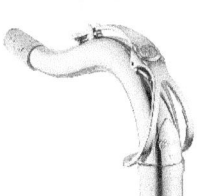	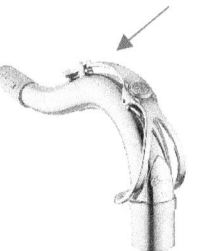	

Pad		Resonator
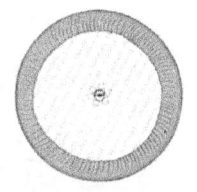		

Tone Hole	Reed	Tenon
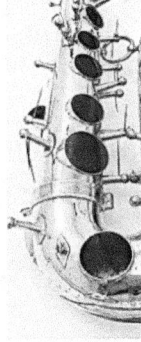		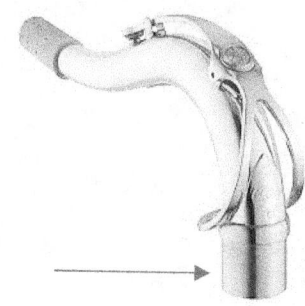

Posts 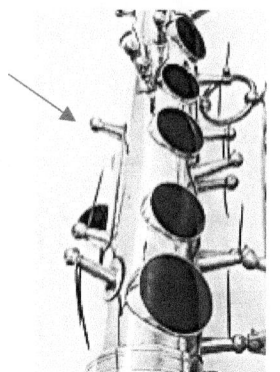 **Springs**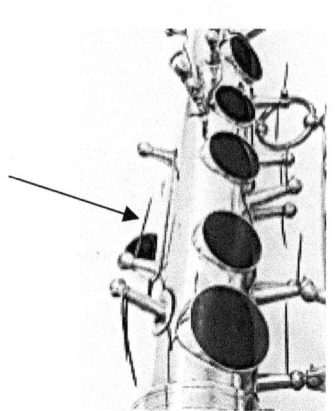

Chapter 2

How Does My Saxophone Work?

Sound Production

The Mouthpiece—Sound is produced on a saxophone by a single cane reed attached by a ligature to a mouthpiece.

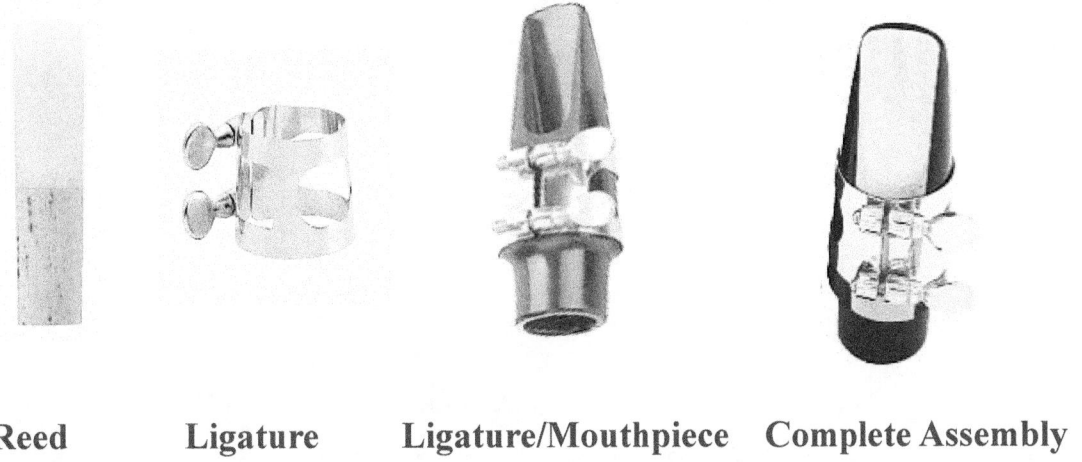

Reed   Ligature   Ligature/Mouthpiece   Complete Assembly

As you send a stream of air against the reed/mouthpiece combination, the reed is set in motion, vibrating against the mouthpiece. This sets the column of air in the instrument's body to vibrate, producing a sound. The quality of that sound is the result of the mouthpiece/reed combination.

The bore of the mouthpiece is the point where the mouthpiece, carrying the "raw" generated sound, meets the bore of the instrument and begins to become a tone. As such, the mouthpiece's bore must match the instrument's bore to allow a smooth, uninterrupted surface for the vibrating column of air to travel into the instrument.

To set up a mouthpiece for use, place the mouthpiece on the neck, place a reed (A) on the flat side of the mouthpiece (B) so that a credit card's thickness of the mouthpiece is showing above the tip of the reed (C).

Place a ligature (D) with the two screws in the back over the reed and mouthpiece to the level of the marking on the mouthpiece. The two screws (E) are on the lower portion of the ligature and reed. Tighten the two screws.

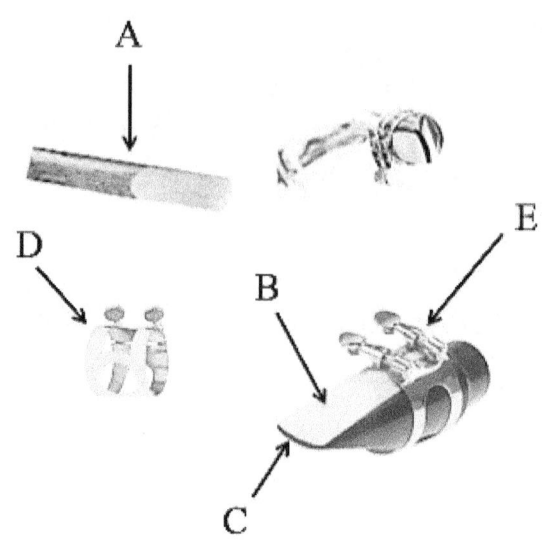

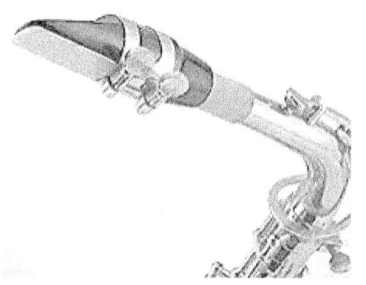

Complete Mouthpiece Ready to Play

Embouchure—The position of your lips and facial muscles when playing your saxophone is called your embouchure. The figure below shows a side view of a mouthpiece facing, which gradually slopes away from the plane of the table. In this area, the reed can vibrate and produce a sound. The reed vibrates from that point up.

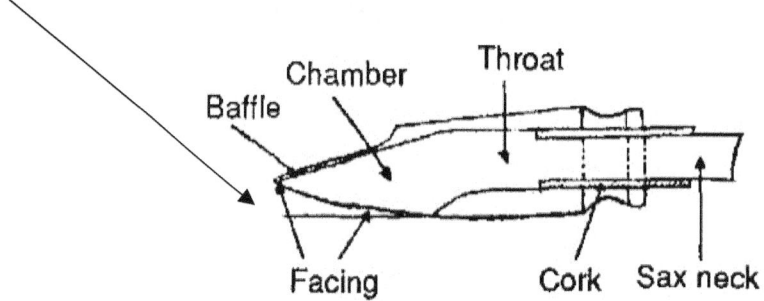

Mouthpiece Facing

Setting your embouchure is a very individual process. It can vary greatly depending on your mouth, dental, and lip structure. The following information is a general description of what is needed for the process. Yours may be different. Always follow the advice of your teacher. To set your embouchure:

1. Pull back your lower lip over your lower teeth just enough to form a pad for the teeth. Too much padding will restrict the reed's vibration.

2. Place the mouthpiece in your mouth with the reed resting on your lower lip at the point where the reed begins to slope away from the lay of the mouthpiece.

3. That point will vary depending on the size and shape of your lips and the shape of your lower teeth. Trial and error will help find the sweet spot to produce a saxophone tone.

4. With your upper teeth firmly on top of your mouthpiece, close your lips around the mouthpiece with a slight smile, keeping the corners of the mouth firm so that no air can escape.

5. Keep your chin muscles firm and pull down.

6. After all the above, blow gently into the mouthpiece, adjusting it slightly in and out of your mouth until a good saxophone sound occurs.

7. Keep your cheek muscles firm when blowing into the mouthpiece to avoid puffy cheeks.

Tuning

Before tuning, a saxophone should be played for a minute to warm it up. To tune your saxophone, twist the mouthpiece slightly in or out of the neck. Moving it in raises the pitch, and moving it out lowers the pitch.

Moving Mouthpiece

Mechanically speaking, this is all you can do to tune a saxophone. However, there are playing adjustments that you can make to improve intonation. The saxophone depends on you, the player, to produce the sound through your embouchure. Learning how to do so can have a great effect on intonation.

Selecting a reed and mouthpiece is important when working for good intonation. These should be chosen with the guidance of your teacher or a saxophone professional. After the selection, playing in tune becomes a matter of embouchure. Tighter or looser embouchures with proper placement of the mouthpiece in the mouth are what control pitch.

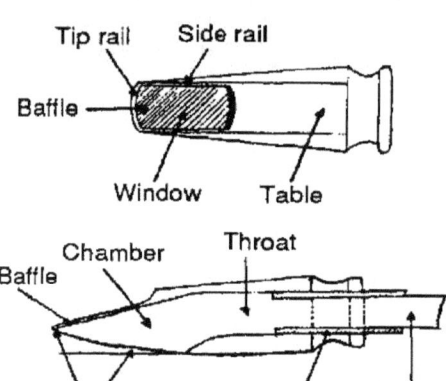

Mouthpiece Parts labeled

The facing is the side where the reed is placed. It is the placement of the reed on the facing that produces the sound. Facing can be short, medium, or long.

Longer facings favor lower sounds.

Shorter facings favor higher sounds.

And medium facings strike a balance.

Medium facing will probably be best for most students.

See Saxophone Mouthpiece Design in the appendix for more information on this topic.

Saxophone Key System

The saxophone key system has the same mechanics as other woodwind instruments, using padded keys to cover the tone holes. A difference in the saxophone pads is that they are usually covered with leather instead of with fish skin or sheepskin used on other woodwind instrument pads. This covering is necessary because the large size of the tone holes and the force of the strike of the keys against the tone holes result in increased wear on the pads. Their large size also makes the pads more likely to collect moisture from your breath, leading to more rapid deterioration. Because leather pads are stronger, they hold up better under those conditions.

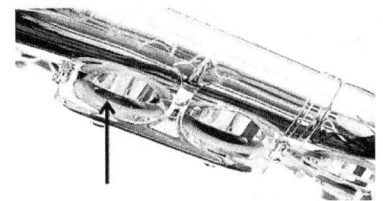 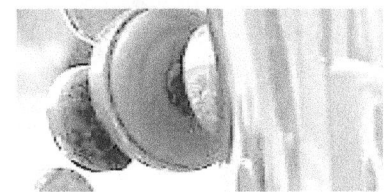

Leather Key Pad

The pads cover 18 to 21 tone holes, depending on the model of the instrument. The tone holes are graduated in size, starting from the top, where the smallest holes are located, to the largest holes at the lowest end of the body. The two vent or octave holes mentioned previously are located nearest the mouthpiece.

Saxophone Tone Holes

The saxophone key system has six tone holes on the front of the instrument's body. Depending on the design of the saxophone, an additional sixteen to eighteen tone holes are placed in different locations to complete the notes on the instrument.

Finger Placement

The six basic tone holes are fingered by your index, middle, and third fingers of each hand. Your left-hand fingers control the upper three keys, and your right-hand fingers control the lower three keys. All the other keys are played by your thumb and pinky finger on each hand and the side of your index fingers.

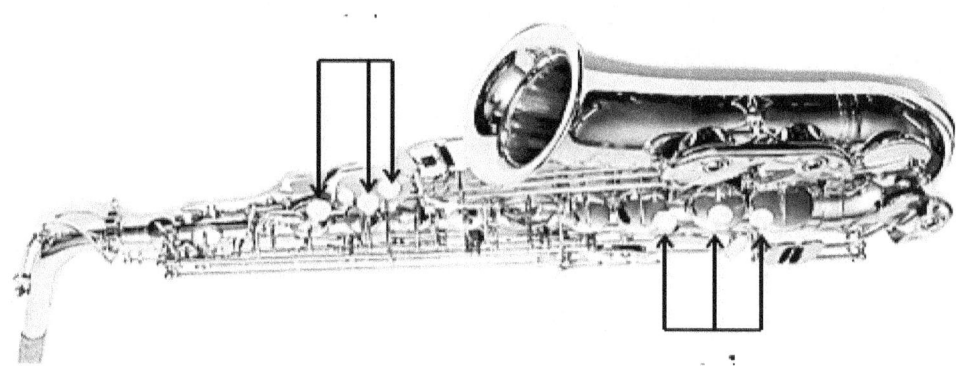

Finger Placement

When playing the saxophone, the sound-producing length of the instrument is as long as the distance between the mouthpiece (A) and the first open hole (B). As you cover the holes by pressing the keys, the instrument becomes longer and the sound lower.

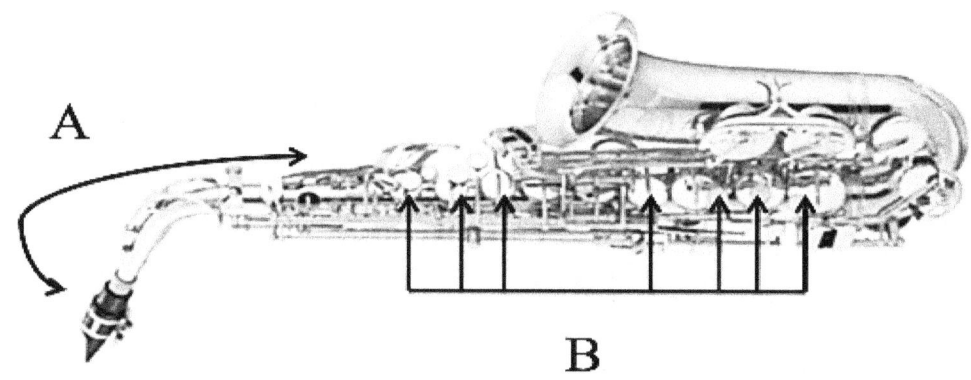

Effective Length

When a saxophone is at rest, some tone holes in the body are closed, and others are open. An open key is one that, when at rest, is not covering the hole it services. That hole is open, but it has a key to cover it when necessary.

Open Key

A closed key refers to a key that, when at rest, covers and seals the hole it services.

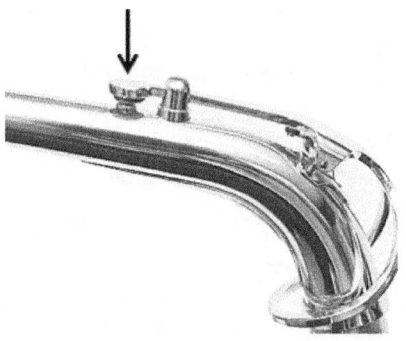

Closed Key

The charts on the following pages show which finger is used for each key, the key system on a saxophone, and a basic fingering chart.

Chart Showing which Finger Is Used for Each Key.

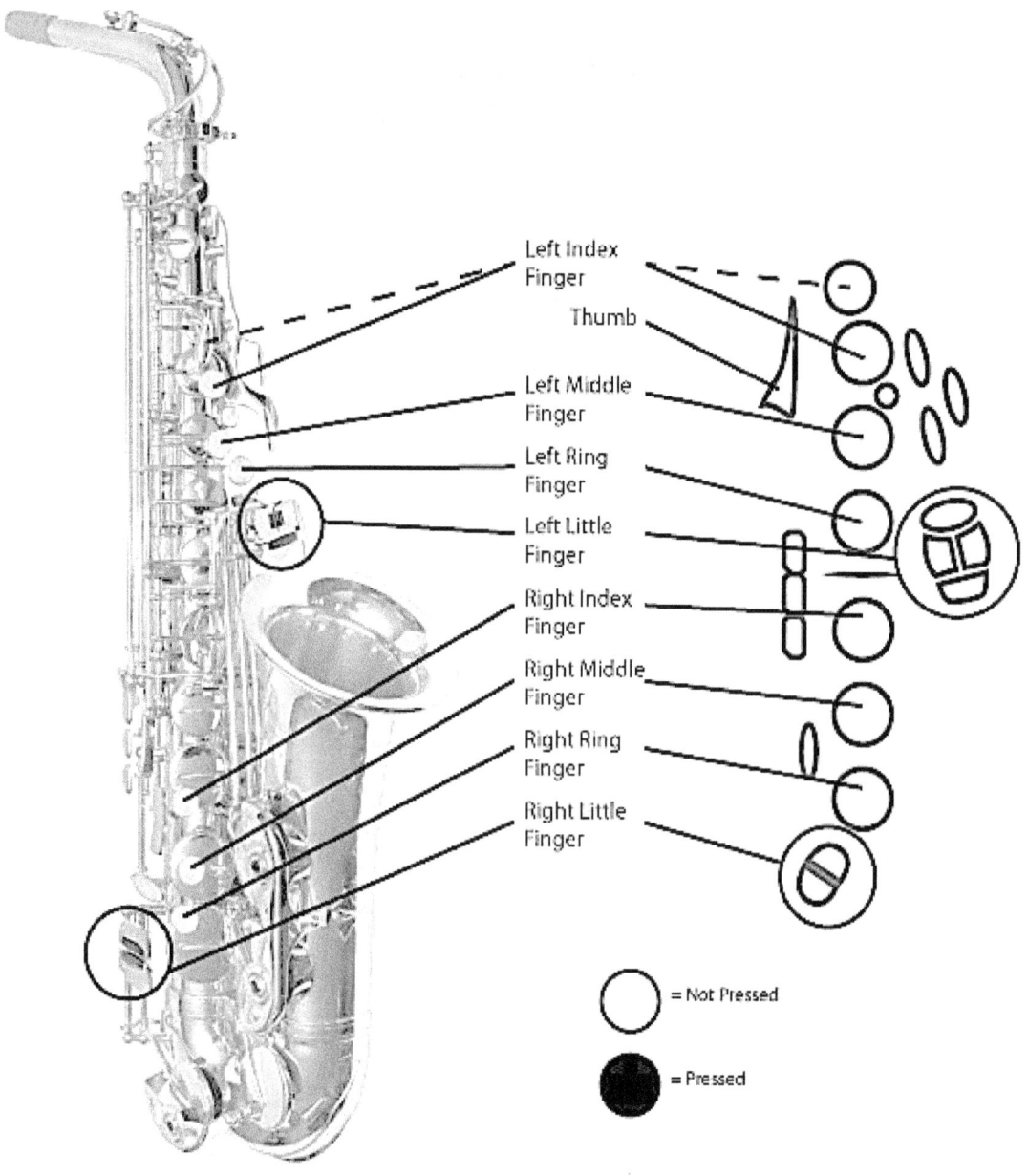

Saxophone Key System

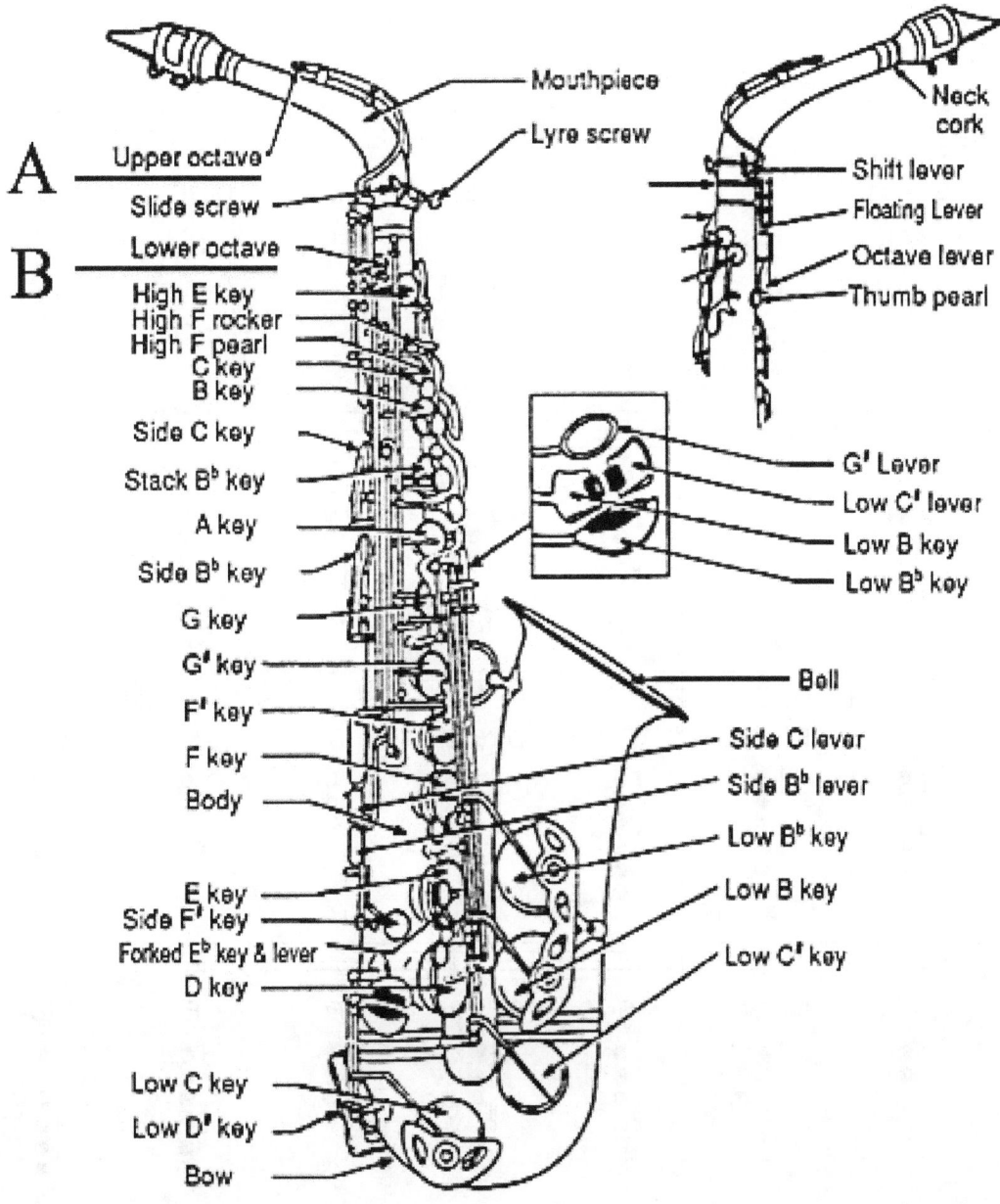

Reproduced with permission from the Brand Instrument Repair Manual by Erick Brand

Basic Saxophone Fingering Chart

To finger a note, press the filled-in keys or levers in the chart. The side keys are pressed by the side of each hand at the first knuckle.

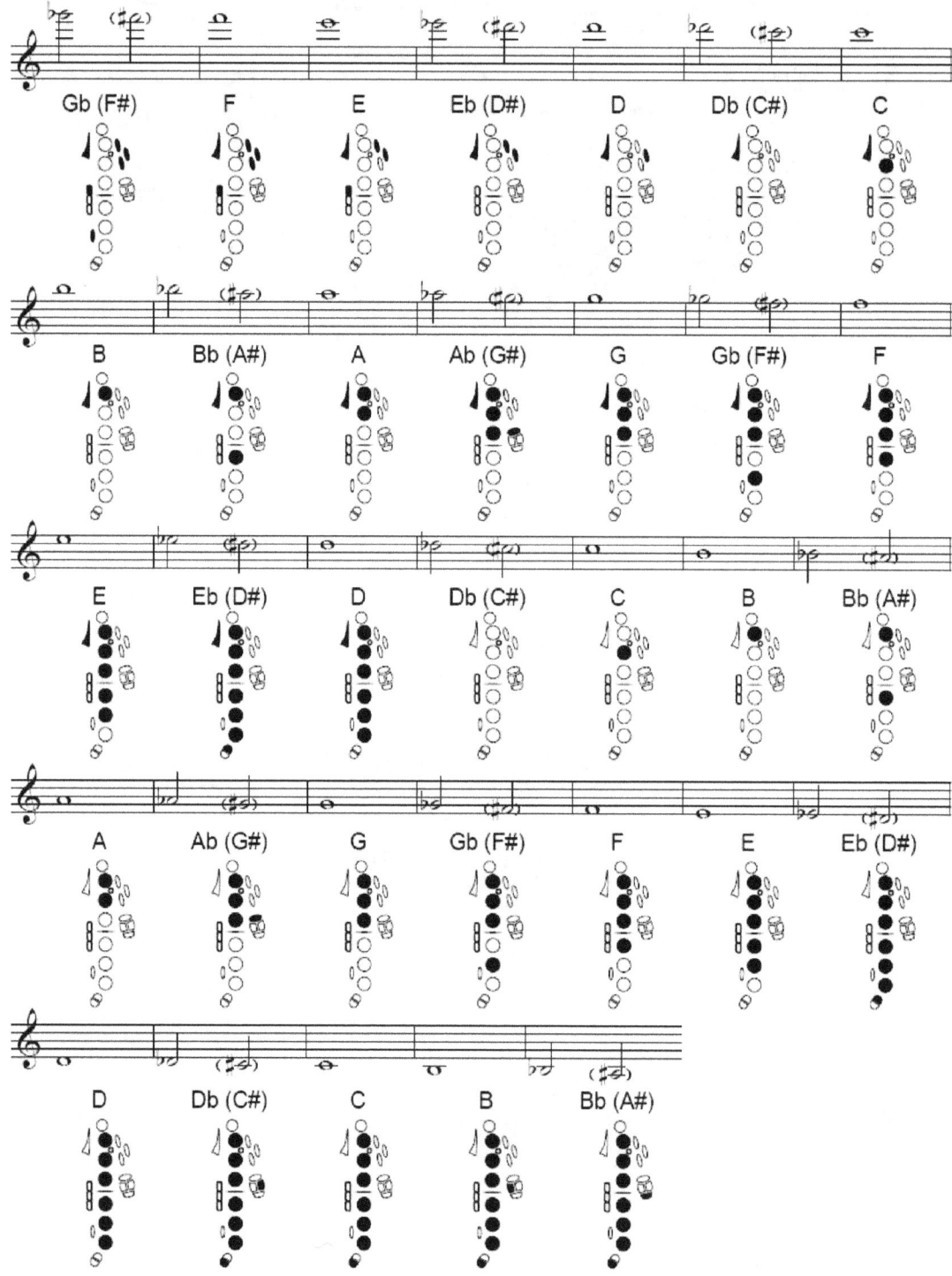

Summary—Because the saxophone is a mechanically complicated instrument, it can have between 22 and 24 keys, each with parts that make those keys function. Your finger placement on those keys and how you work them will control the many notes you will be playing. Your fingering of those keys increases and decreases the vibrating column of air to produce sound. Learning the saxophone's parts and how they work will make you a more rounded musician.

NOTES

Chapter 3

What Are the Different Kinds of Saxophones?

The saxophone bridges the gap between brass and woodwind instruments because it is made of brass but uses a single reed mouthpiece similar to the clarinet.

Saxophones are not usually used in classical music performances; however, some exceptions are found in the works of the composers Sergei Prokofiev and Maurice Ravel. Saxophones are primarily used in jazz, rock, marching, and symphonic bands and as solo instruments or members of a saxophone quartet. The following is an outline of the most popular saxophones used today.

Because saxophones can be inconveniently heavy for many beginning students, several modified versions have been developed to capture that market. In this chapter, you will see references to the tonal range of these instruments written in scientific pitch notation. See the appendix for more on this subject.

Transposing Instruments—Some instruments are called transposing instruments and are referred to as being in a certain key. You will see a Bb clarinet, an Eb saxophone, or an F French horn. These key names refer to the actual note you will hear when the written note C is played on the instrument.

A Review of Transposition—You must understand transposition to determine the exact sound your instrument produces from a written note. A non-transposing instrument will sound as written. The written note C will sound like C. When the written note C is played on a transposing instrument, the note sounded will be the note in the instrument's name. A transposing instrument such as an Eb saxophone will sound an Eb when playing a written C.

Why do different saxophones play in different keys?

A change in the size of an instrument results in a change in the key in which it plays. To increase the range of an instrument, other versions of the same instrument are made in different sizes. Smaller sizes produce notes in higher ranges, and larger sizes produce notes in lower ranges. This arrangement allows you to play these different instruments using the same fingering. The result is these become transposing instruments.

An example in the saxophone family is the Eb sopranino, Bb soprano, Eb alto, Eb contra-alto, Bb tenor, Eb Baritone, Bb Bass, and Eb Contrabass. All these instruments share the same fingerings, so a saxophonist can go from one instrument to another by adjusting to the different instrument's sizes and embouchure.

The sound generators (mouthpiece/ligature/reed), bodies, mechanisms, and acoustical principles are the same for all saxophones. The differences are in size and transposition. The most popular saxophone family members are the soprano, alto, tenor baritone, and bass saxophones. The sopranissimo, sopranino (soprillo), C melody, and contrabass saxophones are other family members not well known.

Soprano Saxophone—The soprano saxophone is a Bb transposing instrument. When you play the note C, it sounds Bb. Also, the notes sound one octave above the tenor saxophone. This instrument is second in size below the sopranino in the saxophone family and has a written range from Ab3 to E6.

The Soprano can be made in three different shapes. One takes the shape of an alto saxophone, although it is smaller. Another shape has a straight body with a bell on the end, like a clarinet. A third shape has a straight body but a curved neck, making it easier to keep a correct embouchure.

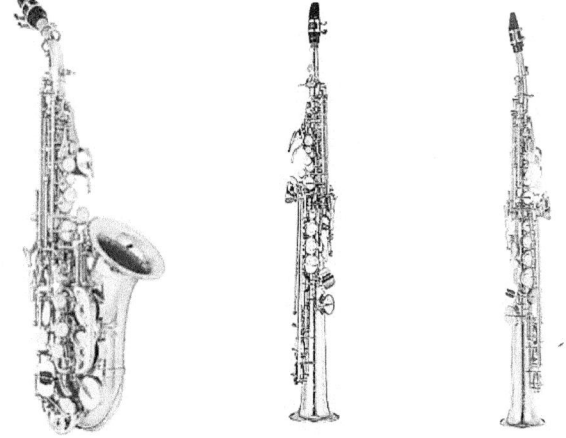

Because of the instrument's small size, the reed and mouthpiece are also small, making it harder to produce good-quality sound and intonation.

Different Shaped Soprano Saxophones

Alto Saxophone—The alto saxophone is the most popular of the family. It transposes in the key of Eb, so you will hear an Eb when you play the written note C. The playing range of the alto saxophone is from Bb3 to F#6. The alto saxophone is mostly used to play jazz, rock, and other types of band music. It is not usually found in the instrumentation of traditional classical music.

Tenor Saxophone—The tenor saxophone is next in line with the saxophone family. Its shape is similar to the alto except for the neck, which is curved to make forming a proper embouchure easier. Its written range is from Ab2 to E5, which lies in the center of the saxophone family of instruments. Because of its size, playing the tenor saxophone requires a bit larger physical effort and the ability to produce a greater airflow. The tenor saxophone is primarily used in a saxophone quartet, jazz, rock, marching, and symphonic bands and occasionally for special instrumentation in a symphony orchestra.

Baritone Saxophone—Eb baritone saxophone is a transposing instrument with a range from C2 to A4. It has the same shape as the alto and tenor but is larger and heavier. The weight of a baritone saxophone can range from 11 to 20 pounds. An extended curved loop leads to the neck and mouthpiece to shorten the height of the instrument.

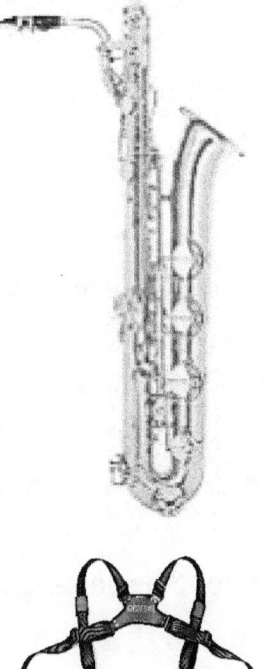

The music for the baritone saxophone is written in the treble clef, sounding an octave and major sixth lower than the written note. The instrument takes its place with the other members of its family in saxophone quartets, jazz and rock music, and symphonic and military marching bands with occasional parts in a symphony orchestra. Because of its weight, special neck straps and harnesses have been designed to help carry the load in marching bands.

Bass Saxophone—Because of its size, the bass saxophone is not popular. Believed to be the first instrument made by the inventor Adolph Sax, he built it to produce an instrument to compete with the force and range of a tuba-like instrument called the ophicleide. The bass saxophone is pitched in the key of Bb and has a range from Ab1 to E4.

The design of the bass saxophone is similar to the alto, tenor, and baritone saxophones, except for the extended looped tubing leading to the mouthpiece. This tubing is necessary for ease of playing by shortening the length of the instrument. Because of its weight and size, the instrument rests on a peg on the floor.

The following saxophones are not popular because of their extraordinary physical characteristics.

Sopranissimo Saxophone—This saxophone is a Bb transposing instrument with a range from Bb4 to F7. The instrument sounds one octave above the soprano. This saxophone is about a foot long with a mouthpiece so small as to make it difficult to control. Because of the small size of the mouthpiece, playing requires a well-developed embouchure.

Sopranino Saxophone is the smallest saxophone, available in straight and curved shapes. The sopranino is a Bb instrument and sounds in the highest range of the saxophone family, an octave above the alto saxophone and two octaves above the baritone. A shortage of music and the instrument's high register make it not particularly popular. The sopranino saxophone has a range from Bb4 to F7.

Saxonette—The saxonette is midway between the clarinet and saxophone. The instrument's body is like a clarinet's upper and lower joints. Joined to that lower portion is a turned-up bell like a saxophone. The saxonette also has a short angular neck designed to make the mouthpiece more convenient for your embouchure. The instrument plays in the key of C with a key system similar to an Albert system clarinet. (See page 51). The body is made of wood and has a clarinet sound.

C Melody Saxophone—In the same non-popular area is the C melody saxophone. Because it plays in the key of C, it is a non-transposing instrument. It can play flute, string instrument music, vocal, and piano arrangements without dealing with transposition issues.

Manufacturing of the C melody ceased decades ago. They are rare but not particularly expensive because a parts shortage makes them difficult to maintain and repair. Mouthpieces and reeds are almost impossible to find, so you can use tenor reeds, but you must use an original C melody saxophone mouthpiece.

Contra Bass Saxophone—The contrabass saxophone is built in the key of Bb and has a range from A3 to F#6. It is the largest and lowest-pitched instrument in the traditional saxophone family. These instruments can weigh as much as forty-five pounds.

Because of its size and weight, it must rest on a peg on the floor when it is played. Its cost (in the $32,000. range) makes it not commonly seen in performance. When used, it would most likely be a jazz or rock ensemble.

Alphasax—One solution to dealing with the size and weight of saxophones can be found with the Eb alphasax. This instrument is designed to satisfy the need for a saxophone that smaller players can handle. The alphasax is 33 percent lighter than the traditional E-flat alto sax and features a traditional body with a key mechanism designed to accommodate smaller hands. The mechanism enables the player to play two octaves chromatically using traditional fingering patterns, allowing the young student to easily prepare for a transition to a traditional saxophone when appropriate.

Saxello—The saxello is a modified form of the soprano saxophone, a Bb instrument designed with a half-upturned bell rather than the traditional bell found on most saxophones. It is believed that the differently shaped bell would improve the tone while directing the sound to the player rather than the audience. The object was to let the player hear the sound more clearly and have a better opportunity to modify it. The saxello was not financially profitable and so had a short history.

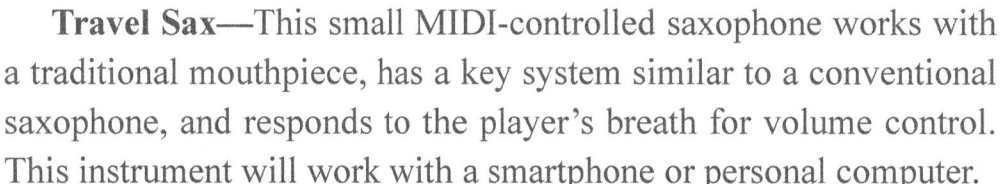

Travel Sax—This small MIDI-controlled saxophone works with a traditional mouthpiece, has a key system similar to a conventional saxophone, and responds to the player's breath for volume control. This instrument will work with a smartphone or personal computer.

Summary—The first model of the saxophone invented by Adolph Sax was the bass saxophone. Numerous models based on that instrument have evolved so that we can now cover the entire range of notes by saxophones, from the sopranino to the contrabass. Additionally, there are saxophone-like instruments, such as the alpha sax and the saxonette, plus numerous other iterations of the original saxophone model.

Chapter 4

How Are Saxophones Made?

The saxophone is an exception to the members of the woodwind family in that its body is made of brass. The process of making a brass body is as follows.

A template marks a form on a sheet of brass that will become a saxophone's bell section. The sheet is cut to a shape that flares out to what appears to be a flattened bell.

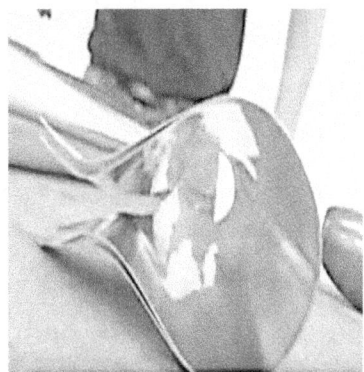

Forming the Saxophone Bell

This form is wrapped around a series of cone-shaped cylindrical rods called mandrels until the brass sheet becomes a saxophone bell.

When a bell shape is made, the craftsman joins the two edges of the sheet. These are notched to make tabs that overlap the seam and form a lap joint to be clipped together.

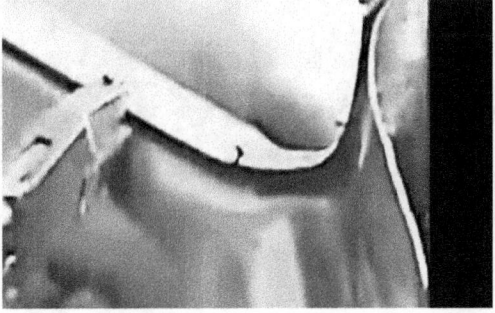

Clipping the Seam

The seam is joined by hammering the overlapping tabs, annealing (heating), and soldering the seam using a brass blend wire melted by a propane torch to about 1500 degrees Fahrenheit to seal it permanently.

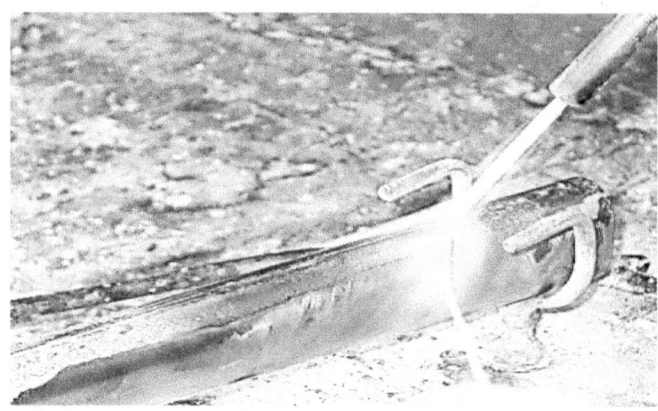

Sealing the Seam
Compliments of Julius Keilwerth's saxophone

After being cooled, the excess brass wire on the seam is hammered down, sanded, and buffed to form a smooth surface.

The bell is transferred to another bell-shaped mandrel, where the brass is further shaped by hammering or mechanical press until the desired bell shape is achieved.

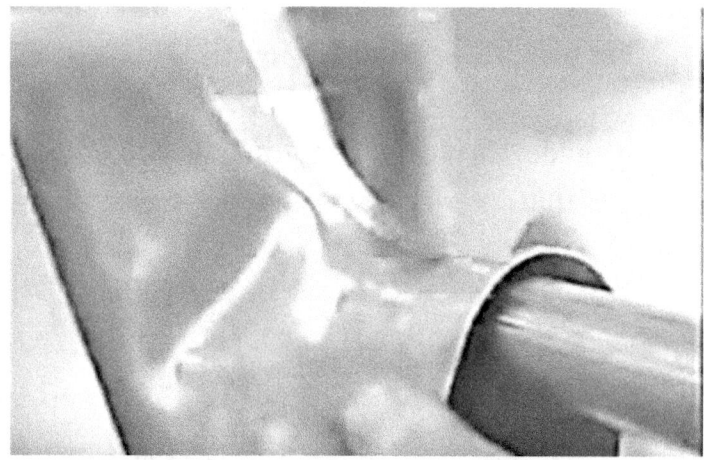

Shaping the Bell

Throughout this procedure, the brass being worked is softened through a process called annealing. When heat is applied to brass, its structure changes at 480 degrees Fahrenheit. As the temperature of the brass continues to rise, the craftsman must control the flow of heat to ensure that the brass reaches but does not exceed the annealing temperature of between 650 and 750 degrees. This can vary depending on the type and thickness of the brass being worked. This process, called eye or hand annealing, allows the maker to judge the exact amount of attention needed for variations in each part of the instrument.

Another method for annealing uses an oven for the process. The instrument is passed through an oven set at a fixed temperature, during which the annealing occurs. This process is effective for mass production purposes; however, it cannot account for the variation in material content and density that the human touch can accommodate. Additionally, using the oven process will subject parts of the instrument to unnecessary heating and cooling.

When the bell is completely formed, a wire rim called a bell bead is placed around its edge, strengthening it to resist denting. The edge of the rim is turned partway outward, forming a pocket into which a brass alloy wire is inserted.

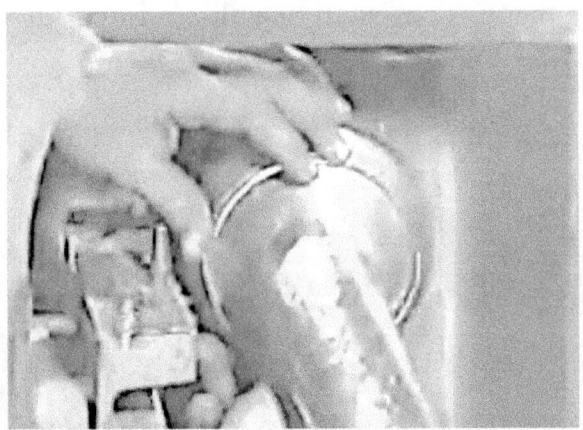

Installing the Bell Bead

The edge of the rim is turned in completely to cover the wire, and the edge is soldered, enclosing the wire. The wire strengthens the rim, adds size to the bell, and affects the bell's resonance depending on the wire's density and how it is installed.

The body of a saxophone contains a series of tone holes placed to satisfy the requirements needed to produce the desired sounds. A conical brass tube is set in a mechanical drill press where pilot holes are drilled. These holes are refined by a process where the metal from around the holes is drawn from the underside upward to form a rough tone hole. These are called drawn tone holes.

Forming Drawn Tone Holes

The tone holes are then refined to a smooth edge upon which padded keys will sit.

With the tone holes complete, the craftsman solders onto the body, posts that will hold the key system in place. These can be soldered directly onto the body individually or soldered onto metal ribs, which will be soldered onto the body.

Direct and Rib Post Construction

Keys—All saxophones have some form of key system. These vary greatly; however, they are made for different woodwind instruments in generally the same way. They can be individually hand-forged by an artisan or mass-produced.

The mass production process for most woodwind instruments begins with making a die for each key. Wax is poured into the die to make a wax mold of the key. The wax key-shaped molds are removed from the die and assembled on a tree-like structure shown below.

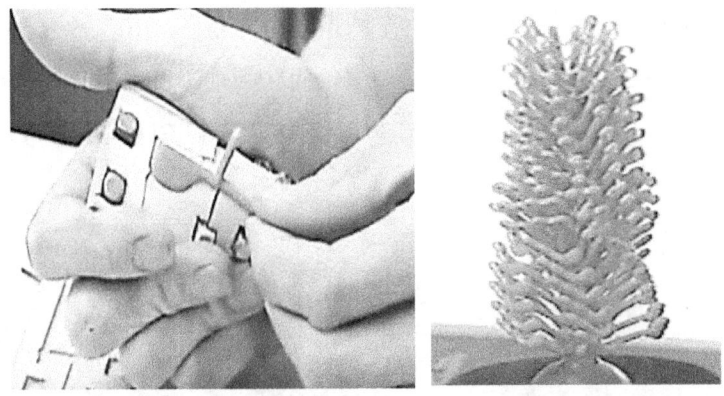

Removing Wax Key from Mold to Make a Key Tree

The tree is placed in a flask filled with plaster that will harden around the tree.

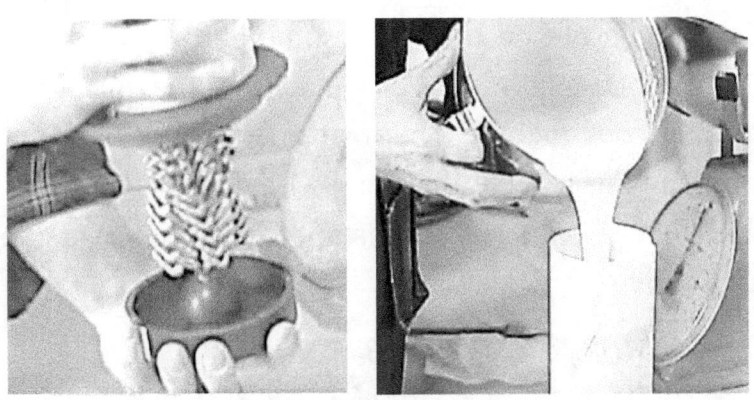

Plaster Cast

After the plaster has hardened around the tree, the wax is melted, and a plaster cast is filled with the molten material used to make the keys. When cooled, the mold is removed, and a tree of metal keys remains. The new key parts are snipped off the tree and soldered together.

Snipping the Keys off the Tree

For hand-forged keys, the metal of choice, usually nickel silver or brass for a saxophone, is used to shape the individual parts of the key. Saxophone pad cups formed from brass are soldered onto arms to form a complete key.

 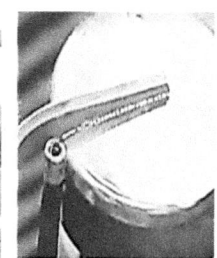  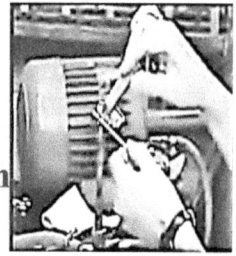

Soldering Pad Cups onto Arms

The keys are polished in preparation for assembly on the instrument. The perfectly clean brass parts are buffed to a high shine and degreased. This procedure removes all substances that may have accumulated on the surface of the body and instrument parts during construction. The instrument's body and its parts are then lacquered. Keys are ready to receive their pads. Leather pads, many of which have resonators (see page 4 for resonators), are installed in the key pad cups using melted shellac or another adhesive.

 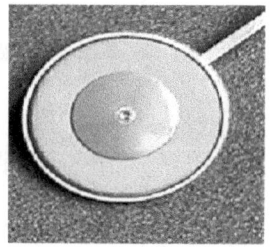

Pad Cup and Pad Cup with Pad

The saxophone is ready to receive the key system when the keys are padded and the posts are in place. The instrument is assembled, the pads are checked for leaks, tested by a professional saxophone player, adjusted as necessary, given a final cleaning, and the saxophone is ready to go.

Summary—Making a saxophone body requires procedures used in making all brass instruments. Making saxophone keys uses techniques used in key making and padding similar to those used in making woodwind instruments. Additionally, as you will read in chapter 7, making the saxophone mouthpiece went through a long and complicated series of trial and error until it reached the assortment of mouthpieces now in use. That being said, the family of saxophones provides a variety of sounds that can vary from warm to assertive and easily blend with any of the other instruments in the orchestra or band.

NOTES

Chapter 5

How Do I Take Care of My Saxophone?

Saxophones require "per-use" care and "periodic" care. Per-use care should take place after each playing session. Periodic care depends on how much time you play your saxophone. Usually, every three months, does the periodic care job.

Mouthpiece Care

Per-Use—After each use:

1. Remove the ligature and reed.
2. Dry the reed on a tissue and put it in your reed case.
3. Use a swab to dry the bore of the mouthpiece.

Periodically—Saxophone mouthpieces can be washed with mild soap and warm water without harmful effects. A mouthpiece brush can be used to get into the mouthpiece bore.

You can also use a commercial disinfectant product specially designed for musical instrument mouthpieces. These are available in most music stores.

Neck Care

Per Use—After each playing session, remove the neck from the body and swab the neck with a saxophone neck swab like the ones pictured.

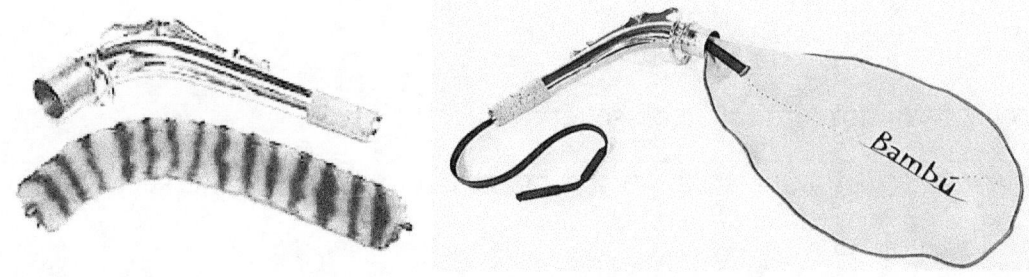

Check the neck cork to decide if it needs additional cork grease.

Periodically—Follow the instructions for periodic body care below.

Bore Care

Per Use—Clean the bore with an appropriate swab after each use. There are many swabs available which will be discussed in chapter 8. You must choose the swab that suits you best, made for your saxophone. Some choices include a simple cloth on a string with a weight on its end to pull through the neck.

The same arrangement with a brush inside the cloth will exert more pressure on the cloth as it passes through the instrument.

Another type will have a chamois in place of the cloth to do the same thing.

A wooden stick covered with microfiber called a pad saver will wipe out the moisture from the bore.

With the neck and mouthpiece off:

1. Swab the mouthpiece as described above.

2. Pass a neck swab through the neck several times.

3. Pass your swab of choice through the bore several times to be sure you have removed all the moisture.

4. If you use a "bore saver" swab, leave it in the instrument.

Periodically—Wipe the major body sections that do not have keys with a soft, damp cloth. With a dry cloth, wipe the same area again to remove any moisture. Do not use any liquid polish.

Key Care

Per Use—The parts of the keys that come into contact with your fingers should be cleaned regularly. Under no circumstances should any liquid polish be used on keys. It is unnecessary, can harm the keys' motion, and might damage the key's finish and the pads. A wipe with your cloth of choice will do the job.

1. Wash your hands before you begin to play.
2. Using a soft cloth, gently wipe the surface of the keys that your fingers touch as you play.
3. Wipe the keys back to front toward you, never side to side.

Periodically—Use a soft-bristle brush, such as those used for makeup, and brush off the lint and residue that may collect between the keys. If there is anything the brush will not remove, use a Q-tip. Be careful not to displace a spring or damage a pad during this process.

The next issue of importance in key maintenance is lubrication. Depending on use, the age of the instrument, and the environment in which it lives, make a judgment as to how often lubrication is needed, but be flexible since conditions such as climate, use, and locations may change during different periods throughout the year. Common sense without rigidity in decision-making is always the best route to take.

Selecting Key Oil—To decide how long an oil will work successfully before evaporating, rub a drop of oil between your thumb and index finger and judge how long the oily sensation lasts. Compare several oils against one another. Petroleum-based oils will probably last a shorter time than synthetic oils. The choice of oil is a very individual one.

Light oil evaporates more quickly than thicker oils. Light oil tends to travel down the post to the instrument's body. This is messy and will collect dust.

To test the viscosity (thickness) of oil, shake the bottle to see how the contents moves. The slower the oil moves, the thicker it is. To compare the thickness of several oils, place a drop of each, side by side, on one end of a smooth, flat surface. Then, raise that end of the surface and note the rate of speed at which the oils travel downward. Thicker oils will move more slowly. With several choices, try each on one saxophone key using a different key for each trial. Do not combine different oils during the trial.

Using Oil—The figure below shows key oil in a needle-type dispenser for easy distribution. The oil you use for each process will have to be your decision. Use the following information to start your search on the subject. The oils that are packaged with a needle applicator are very convenient.

Key Oil

The Process—Key oil is needed to prevent rust, quiet the key's action, and lubricate the key's moving parts. Keys are held on a saxophone's body by posts through which a pivot screw or rod is inserted to hold the key in place. These screws are connected to the key barrel, a tube on which a pivot screw holds the key from both sides.

Oiling keys is a simple process. "Less is more." The amount of oil and how often it should be used should be minimal.

1. Use the applicator tip on a bottle to apply the smallest amount of oil possible to both sides of the key barrel at every point where a key that moves is connected to the instrument's posts.

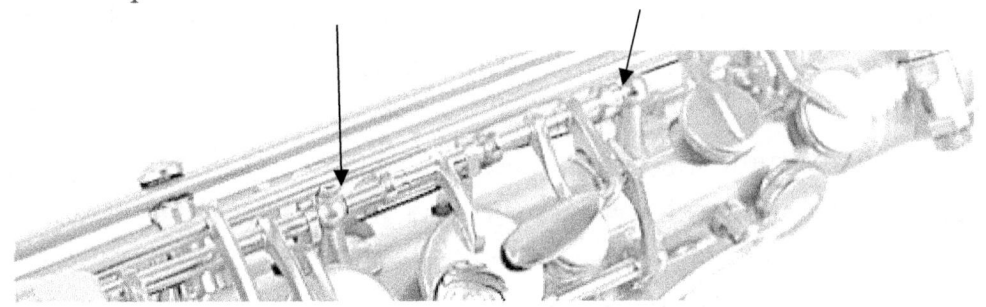

Oiling Posts

2. As you oil, work the key up and down to help the oil travel into the barrel.

3. Deciding how often it is necessary to do this depends on your instrument use. Be flexible about that timing decision should your use of the instrument change.

4. You must take greater action if a key's operation is sluggish or won't move. If you have any mechanical ability, this will be an easy job. If you consider yourself to be a "call the man" type, by all means, bring the instrument to a certified repair person.

To deal with a stuck screw, you will need a flat surface on which to work, an appropriate size saxophone screwdriver, a needle nose plyer, a large absorbent cloth, a smaller absorbent cloth, isopropyl alcohol, pipe cleaners, penetrating oil, and the key oil of choice. You will be working on the soft cloth spread on a flat surface. A bath towel is best.

1. Spread the towel out on a flat surface.

2. Place the instrument on the towel.

3. Use a soft-bristle brush to remove all the lint and dust accumulated within the key system.

4. Put a drop of oil on both sides of the barrel of the problem key where it joins the post.

5. Work the key up and down until it moves more easily than it did previously.

6. Loosen and then retighten the screw.

   Should the screw or rod be rusted or bound in place, use a single drop of penetrating oil at the contact points. Let the penetrating oil remain for 15 minutes while you work the key up and down periodically. Make every effort not to get the penetrating oil on the instrument's body. When you feel enough time has passed, try to <u>tighten</u> the screw the tiniest bit to break the bind. Then try again to loosen the screw. During this process, you must use a screwdriver that is a perfect fit for that screw slot to help prevent stripping the screw. If you cannot move the screw, bring it to a professional.

7. If you are removing a pivot screw, it should come out easily. If it is a rod screw, after the thread clicks, indicating it is totally unscrewed, remove the screw with the needle nose plyer. The key will come out of place, but it is easy to replace after the screw is cleaned.

8. Clean the rod screw with alcohol on the small rag.

9. Pass an alcohol-moistened pipe cleaner through the key's barrel.

10. Pass an oil-moistened pipe cleaner through the key's barrel.

11. Return the key to its original position and replace the screw.

   If you find rust on the key springs during this process, use a Q-tip to swab the affected spring with some oil.

   Sticking Pads—The best solution to sticking pads is preventing it from happening. If you, as the player, avoid any food or drink other than water one hour before playing your instrument, the likelihood of your pads' sticking will greatly diminish.

When you eat or drink, other than water, your breath carries minute particles of food and vapors that contain anything in your mouth at the time, through your instrument and onto its pads. If you do not eat or drink, there is still some small chance of sticking pads caused by the moisture that the pads will inevitably pick up, combined with dust and residues of any kind in the environment.

Another cause of sticking pads can be any key oil seepage that might migrate to the tone hole edges and then to the pads. To avoid this situation, you must follow the "less is more" rule when applying oil to your instrument.

Treatment —Before treating a sticking pad, be sure a weak spring is not the cause of the problem. Bending the spring slightly in the same direction it already takes can make a significant difference. If that does not help, proceed with the pad cleaning process.

Holding the instrument with the offending key located next to your ear, work the key. If the pad is sticky, you will hear a subtle clicking sound showing the pad sticking to the tone hole. If that sound is present, move on to treating the pad. There are several ways to treat a sticking pad.

If the pad is old or showing signs of wear, the best solution is to remove the key, clean the tone hole edge with alcohol, and replace the pad with a new one.

If the pad is in good condition and the tone hole edge is clean, you might want to try some of the remedies on the market. There are various pad cleaning papers that you can place between the offending key and its tone hole. Place the paper between the keypad and the tone hole, gently close the key onto the paper, and withdraw it.

Another option is using keypad powders, which are supposed to remedy the sticky pad problem when applied to the pad.

Some technicians recommend swabbing the pad with a Q-tip moistened in lighter fluid. Others suggest the same process using isopropyl alcohol.

The opponents of these methods claim that the paper products will damage the pads, the powders will build up on the pad, and worsen the problem. You should draw your own conclusion.

Case Care

Caring for your saxophone case is simple.

Per Use—Don't put anything in the case that is not a saxophone.

Periodically—Vacuum the inside occasionally.

Clean the outside of the case with a damp cloth.

If the case is a hard shell, when the outside of the case is dry, use the spray wax of your choice to finish the job.

If the case is canvas-covered, stop there.

Summary—Saxophone maintenance is labor-intensive because of its numerous parts and complicated mechanism. You will find many opinions on how these instruments should be maintained. Your best direction would be to evaluate how often and where it is used, where and for how long it is stored without use, the climate in which you live, and whatever directions were included with the original packaging if the instrument was purchased new.

Trial and error in selecting the products will eventually bring you suitable equipment and materials for your situation. As a rule, move thoughtfully, slowly, and intelligently, and remember that less is more.

Chapter 6

How Should I Plan My Practice Sessions?

You have heard the old saying that "practice makes perfect." Well, practice can make perfect, but only if you practice with understanding, patience, and the will to "get it right."

Playing an exercise or musical selection often will make it better only if you understand how the piece should sound and know how to make it sound that way. Playing a piece incorrectly repeatedly can result in your learning to play it wrong well. Here are some suggestions that will help you get the best results from your practice period:

1. Select a place in your home where you can practice without disturbing your family and where their daily life will not distract you from your work.

2. Pick a practice time that comfortably fits your daily study schedule. Try to use that same time each day.

3. Set a long-term general goal. Then, set some short-term goals to help you reach the long-term goal. Choose a topic like tone quality, intonation, phrasing, and dexterity (moving your fingers fast) as some of these short-term goals. Then, apply them to your long-term goal of making beautiful music beautifully.

4. Have a plan for each practice period. What part of your long-term goal do you want to accomplish in each period? For example, "Today, I will work on tone quality and embouchure."

5. How long and how often should you practice? Daily practice is best. However, how long you practice should vary with your short-term goal. Shorter daily practice periods produce better results than less frequent long sessions.

6. After you have set your goal and begun to practice, decide on the amount of time and how often you will need to practice to achieve each target.

7. Discuss your plans with your teacher, who can help you make the plan and your goal.

8. Equipment—You must have all the necessary equipment for a successful practice period. Your equipment should include a music stand, metronome, chair if you plan to sit, cleaning cloth, saxophone swabs, and whatever else you feel you need to be comfortable.

Breathing—Before planning your practice sessions, think about your breath as the source of the sound you will make on your saxophone.

A muscle that separates your lungs from your stomach area controls your normal breathing process. This muscle is called a diaphragm. As you breathe, your diaphragm moves up and down. When it moves down, it increases the area in your lung cavity, causing a vacuum that your lungs fill by drawing in air. When the diaphragm moves up, the lung cavity is smaller, and the air in your lungs is pushed out. You can see a great animated example of diaphragmatic breathing on Wikipedia. Search *diaphragmatic breathing* and look at the right-hand side of the first page for the diagram.

As a saxophone player, one of the most important skills you must master is controlling your diaphragm and, in so doing, controlling your airflow, which is the fuel supply for the tone you produce on your saxophone. Your diaphragm is regulated by your ABS (abdominal muscles). Expanding and contracting those muscles allows you to move your diaphragm up or down.

Try this! Lie down on a flat surface and relax. Place a book on your abdomen and breathe in and out. As you do so, you will notice that the book on your abdomen will rise and fall as you breathe. When you breathe in, the book will rise; as you breathe out, the book will fall.

Now breathe out all the air in your lungs by contracting your ABS. Then take a deep breath in by expanding your ABS. Do not move any other part of your body, such as raising your shoulders or expanding your chest. Raising your shoulders does nothing, and your chest will expand itself as your lungs fill with air. This expansion and contraction of your abdominal muscles is called diaphragmatic breathing. It is something you do all day long without thinking about it.

To apply this procedure to playing the saxophone, you must take a deep breath by expanding your diaphragm as much as possible. Remember not to expand your chest or raise your shoulders. Your lungs should be full of air.

Now, let the air out through pursed lips or by playing a long tone on your saxophone. As you begin to run out of air, put an extra push on your ABS, and you will notice that there will still be a bit more air left to use. Practice this process regularly to develop breath control. The better you control your airflow through "conscious diaphragmatic breathing," the greater the fuel supply you will have for your embouchure.

The Process—You can use the following ideas to make your practice period productive.

1. Warm up with some simple scales using long tones that start very softly (pianissimo—*ppp*), increase in volume (crescendo) to a full sound (forte—*fff*), and then gradually diminish the sound (diminuendo or dim.) back to the original *ppp*. Listen as you play. Are you playing in tune and with the best tone quality you can produce?

2. After warming up with some long tones, add some rhythmic patterns of your creation to those same scales. Listen carefully to intonation as you play. Playing in tune is a must for any saxophonist.

3. As you advance, you can expand the warmup material to include exercises.

4. Follow your warmup by playing a tune that you like. Enjoy the music.

5. Improvisation is fun. Make up your own tune or try to play a tune "by ear." No need for printed music here.

6. Start practicing the material your teacher assigned in your last lesson. Follow the instructions carefully. Listen to yourself, sing the music before you play it, feel the rhythm, and be sure you are playing in tune.

7. Record yourself on your cell phone as you play. Then listen to the recording and be very critical of your intonation, phrasing, and general musicianship.

8. Did you like what you heard? If your answer is yes—great! If it is not, think of what you did not like. Figure out how you can make it better. Then, make it better. Check again to be sure you are playing in tune, using a proper embouchure and phrasing. Are you keeping a proper playing position?

Apps and Your Cell Phone—Using your cell phone or computer, you can search for "Apps for saxophone practice." You will find many that are free and will help you practice better. Some sites also have free music that you can print. Others show playing techniques and play-a-long sessions where you join others to play saxophone music. Use the same search on YouTube to find many sites you will enjoy watching while learning about playing and caring for your saxophone.

Summary—Developing a structure for your practice sessions that works for you will increase your level of achievement. Playing "stuff" without a plan may be fun but does not encourage learning. If you are building a brick wall, you must begin with a solid foundation on which the wall will rest. Your practice periods are the foundation upon which your performance will rest.

Chapter 7

A Survey of the History of Woodwind Instruments

The Flute—The flute results from 43,000 years of history. It probably all began in Slovenia, a European country bordering Italy. In Slovenia, a cave bear's femur (thighbone) carved to look like a primitive flute with several tone holes was discovered. Another such instrument made from a vulture's wing bone was found in Germany. That instrument is estimated to be about 35,000 years old. These and other objects tell us that very early on, humankind was becoming aware that a stream of air passing through a tube could produce sound.

Simple flute-like instruments dating back to the pre-Christian era have been discovered in numerous countries. Instruments made from crane bones dated 9000 years old and others made of bamboo from 433 B.C. were discovered in China. Below are some examples of primitive wind instruments. Search Google Images Primitive Flutes to see many other examples.

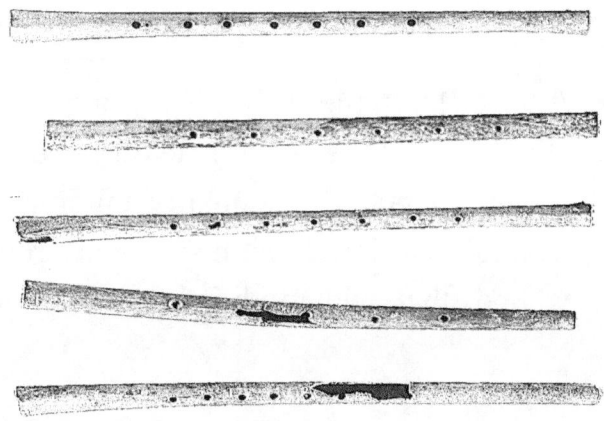

Below is a picture of today's modern flute. Quite a difference!

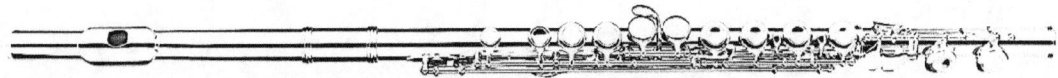

In 2004 in southern Germany, an instrument made from a mammoth tusk and two other instruments made from swan bones were discovered. Similar instruments have been found in many locations throughout the world. This tells us that there is no absolute way to assign an accurate time or location to the "invention" of the flute. We must be satisfied with the theory that the flute evolved along with the development of humankind.

By the sixteenth century, the flute had been developed into a one-piece cylinder with six tone holes. Covering the holes with the fingers allowed the player to produce different notes within a limited range. To make up for that limitation, the instruments were made in different sizes, producing different pitches. Larger instruments produced lower sounds, while smaller instruments produced higher sounds. That progress reached a point in the eighteenth century when flute makers began to develop key systems. As a result, we now enjoy the flute we use today.

Jacques-Martin Hotteterre (1674–1763), renowned flutist and instrument maker of the time, is credited with improving the transverse flute by devising the three-piece design with a separate head joint, body, and foot joint structure. From that period on through the early eighteen-hundreds, improvements were made by relocating and resizing the six-tone holes and adding keys. This all resulted in improved intonation and a greater capability to perform chromatics.

Theobald Boehm (1794–1881), In the early 1800s, Boehm, a jeweler, and goldsmith, an accomplished flutist and flute maker, determined that larger, properly spaced tone holes would produce a better tone quality and improved intonation. For approximately twenty years, he redesigned the instrument producing a key system on a three-piece cylindrical body that, with modifications, became the instrument we know today.

The following is a timeline for the evolution of the flute.

1000–1400—The Medieval period in world history. The beginnings of society as we now know it.

Below is a reproduction of an instrument that was called a flute during the years 1000 through 1400. Look at the end of the instrument, and you will see no embouchure hole like the one on a flute. In its place is a cut in the wood, which makes a sharp edge (arrow) against which the air blown into the instrument strikes and produces a sound. This type of sound-maker is called a fipple.

Compare the fipple to the flute embouchure hole pictured below.

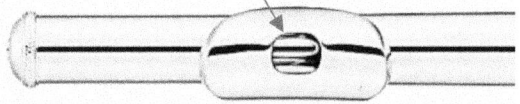

A flute player must direct a stream of air against the edge (arrow) of the flute's embouchure hole. In a fipple instrument, the air stream is directed to the exact spot. You might be familiar with a recorder instrument pictured below. A recorder is a fipple instrument.

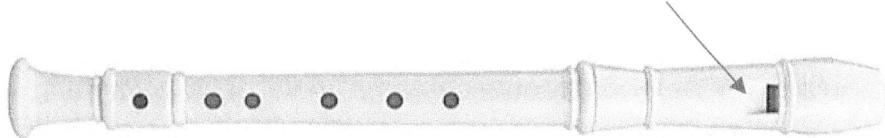

The early instruments, called flutes, had no keys and six equally spaced tone holes. We now name these fipple instruments recorders.

1400–1600—The Renaissance Period in World History. A period of reawakening where society began to understand art, science, and music.

Adding an embouchure hole and spacing the tone holes in two sets of three was the next step in developing the flute and the clarinet. These instruments had a better-sounding upper register but were still not great in the lower notes.

1600–1760—The Baroque Period in World History. A period when music, art, architecture, and the general style of living became very elaborate and highly crafted. Much music was written with several complicated, layered melodies at the same time. This is called counterpoint.

During these years, the flute was divided into four and three sections. The bore (inside tube) was tapered, larger at the embouchure hole, and gradually smaller toward the end. With these adjustments, the flute sound improved and could be tuned.

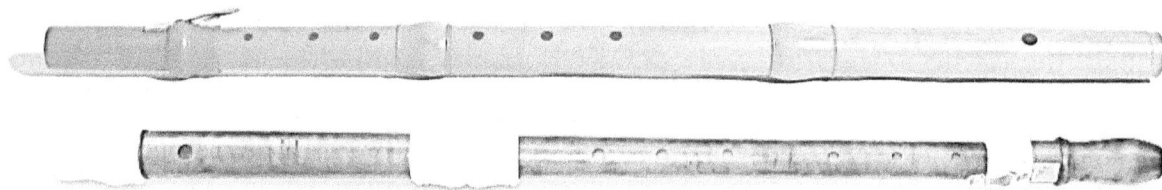

1760–1820—The Classical Period in World History. A period when music and the arts became simpler, and music was written with a single melody and harmony (chords). The flute becomes a part of the orchestra with music by Haydn, Mozart, and Beethoven.

George Catlin (1778–1852), a musical instrument maker, made a variety of experimental flutes beginning with one key and gradually adding keys. These additional keys improved the intonation of the instruments and made it possible for a flute player to play more notes with greater ease.

Rick Wilson's Historical Flute Page http://www.oldflutes.com/boehm.htm is a great source of information on the flute's history. Below is a picture of two early Boehm flutes from Rick Wilson's website.

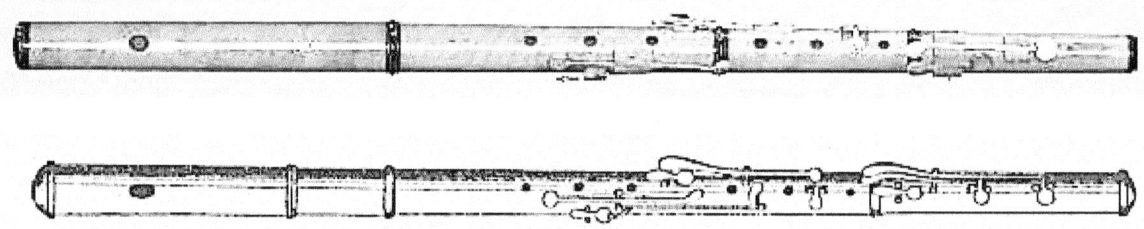

Rick Wilson indicates that these photos and essays may be copied for personal use or used in moderation on web pages, etc., as long as he is clearly acknowledged as the source. All but minimal use of the photos or essays on the web should be accompanied by a link to these pages.

The following is a survey of the history of the other most popular woodwind instruments now in use: the clarinet, saxophone, oboe, and bassoon. You will read about instruments that preceded those, some by several thousand years. Other instruments, such as the saxophone, invented at a known time in music history, will receive a more accurate account of their development.

The aulos is perhaps the flute-like instrument most frequently represented in ancient Greek illustrations, literature, and the Bible. Dating as far back as the sixth century B.C., the aulos was used as an accompaniment to vocal performers and as a solo instrument. The primary settings for their use extended to festive occasions of all kinds, athletic events, and funerals. Originally made of various kinds of wood, such as cane or boxwood, more sophisticated bronze, bone, and ivory models appeared.

One version of the aulos was constructed with two pipes, each with a double reed as its sound generator. Different illustrations show the instrument as two units held individually while being played simultaneously. Variations of the aulos will have five to seven tone holes on each pipe, and more advanced models with a ring-type device at the top of the pipes. This was used to alter the pitch.

In 1921, twenty-three feet of tubing and assorted fragments were discovered in the tomb of Queen Amanishakheto in Meroe, Sudan. These are believed to be sections of different types of auloi that were parts of a professional musician's equipment.

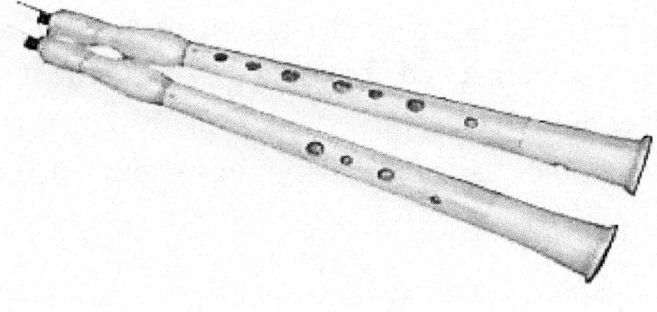

Aulos

Windcap Instruments

Using a windcap instrument, the player blew through a hole in the top of the windcap and, in so doing, activated the double reed inside. The disadvantage of a windcap sound generator is the player's lack of control over the action of the reed other than to start, increase, or decrease volume to some degree and to stop the sound. All the nuances of pitch, volume, and timbre associated with a player's contact with a reed are lost in a windcap instrument.

Windcap

The Zummara —The zummara, native to Egypt, had a windcap sound generator. The instrument had two pipes, one functioning as a drone supplying a continuous underlying tone. The other pipe was used to play the melody. The player was required to finger both pipes by spanning the holes on each pipe simultaneously. The intonation was dreadful.

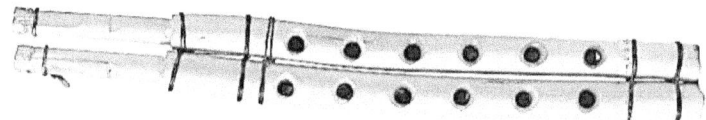

Zummara

The Crumhorn—The crumhorn (curved horn) appeared in Germany in the late fourteenth century and maintained its popularity in Germany, Italy, and the surrounding areas for about three centuries. As a windcap instrument, the player blew through a hole in the top of the windcap and, in so doing, activated the double reed inside.

The crumhorn was constructed with a cylindrical bore similar to a clarinet. This resulted in the instrument's overblowing (raising the register) at the twelfth instead of an octave at which a conical bore instrument would sound. The crumhorn had fingering like the clarinet's chalumeau (lowest) register but was limited to about an octave. The instrument was difficult to play in the upper range, had a somewhat raucous sound, and did not excel in pitch accuracy. Below is a picture of a crumhorn and a breakdown of its windcap reed unit.

Crumhorn

Single Reed Instruments

Single-reed instruments of the idioglot version, where the reed is carved from part of the instrument, date back to three thousand B.C.

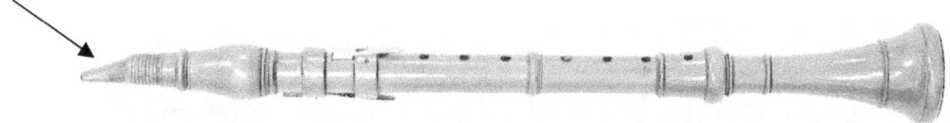

We might speculate that these instruments were the precursors of the clarinet and saxophone.

The Chalumeau—Chalumeau (chalumeaux plural) was used throughout central Europe as early as the twelfth century. The early chalumeau lacked musical sophistication in intonation and tone quality, so its use and repertoire were relegated to folk rather than classical compositions.

Eventually, improvements were made to the instrument so that by 1700, the chalumeau evolved into a single reed woodwind instrument with six tone holes, one key on the front, and one hole on the back. Its range, from F3 below middle C to A4 above middle C, was equal to that of the present-day clarinet's lower so-called chalumeau register. This more sophisticated chalumeau gained acceptance throughout France and Germany and became part of the popular instrumentation.

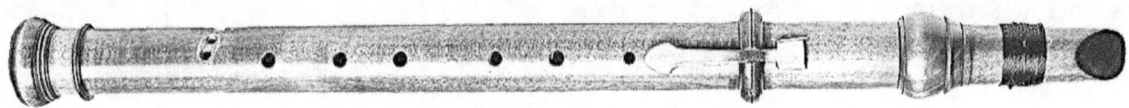

Chalumeau

Because the chalumeau had a range of only twelve notes, the players were required to use as many as four different models to cover the range from F3, a fifth below middle C, to Bb5 above the treble staff. At this time, eight original chalumeaux are in existence. These are models for contemporary makers who produce chalumeaux to satisfy the present market.

The Clarinet

John Christoph Denner (1655–1707), an instrument maker, along with his son Jacob, is credited with advancing the technology of the chalumeau by first adding two keys and then gradually changing the size of the tone holes to improve intonation. Denner then relocated and added keys and a bell, increasing the length of the instrument. The result was a clarinet with an extended range to include the higher (clarion) register.

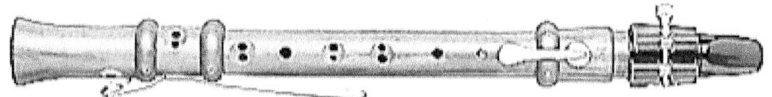

Early Clarinet

In the Middle Ages, the word clarion was applied to the trumpet. Because notes played on the clarinet in the upper register paralleled the intensity of those of a trumpet, the term was applied to that clarinet register. Combined with the chalumeau or lower register and eventually extending the range up to the altissimo, higher register, by 1800, the clarinet became the single reed instrument of choice, relegating the chalumeau instrument to a lesser status.

From then on, a series of artist/instrument makers modified the instrument over 300 years to the point where it is now the contemporary clarinet. During that period, Ivan Muller, Hyacinthe Klosé, Auguste Buffet, Theobald Boehm, Heinrich Joseph Baermann, Eugène Albert, and Adolphe Sax each contributed modifications that would result in the contemporary clarinet with a key system consisting of 17 to 22 keys and 4 to 6 rings.

Ivan Müller (1786–1854) invented the air-tight pad, making possible the addition of enough keys to facilitate playing chromatics on the clarinet. Müller pads replaced the flat brass keys with leather pads that did not cover the tone holes. Müller also invented the metal ligature, which replaced the string or wire used up to that point to secure the reed to the mouthpiece. An interesting note is that, to date, some clarinetists still prefer the use of string in place of a ligature.

In addition to inventing the air-tight pad and the ligature, Müller redesigned the clarinet to contain thirteen keys to service redesigned tone holes. The result was a greater facility for the player and improved intonation. Müller's system had no ring keys.

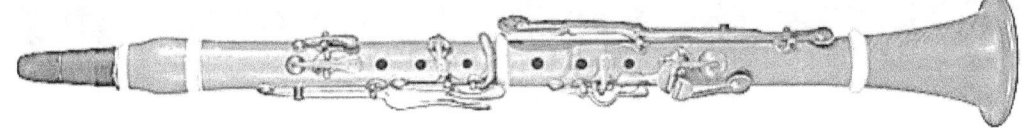

Müller System Clarinet

Eugene Albert (1816–1890) was a Belgian clarinet maker who developed a key system based on the Müller 13 key system but with the addition of two ring keys. Adolphe Sax, a clarinet maker and saxophone inventor, was Albert's tutor. Sax was responsible for adding the two ring keys to Albert's key system. After that, Albert added two more rings, resulting in the "Albert System" with thirteen keys and four ring keys. This arrangement enhanced the intonation of the clarinet and once again made fingering and cross-fingering easier.

Albert's clarinets were very well received because of their excellent craftsmanship and intonation; however, there was one limitation. The instruments were made to pitch A=452 vibrations per second, meaning that the general intonation was higher than the standard A=440. Albert's son, also a clarinet maker, seeing his father's instruments going out of favor, built a clarinet to tune to A=440, extending the popularity of the Albert System clarinets into the twentieth century.

Albert System Clarinet

Hyacinthe Klosé (1808–1880), August Buffet (1789–1864), and the Boehm System—The Boehm key system, originally invented by Theobold Boehm for the flute, served as a model for Hyacinthe Klosé and August Buffet to create a key system for the clarinet. Over about four years, starting in 1839, they modified ring keys and side keys, enabling clarinetists to pay chromatics and difficult passages with comparative ease and a much-improved intonation. Theobold Boehm had no part in this transition except to have been the inspiration for what is called the Boehm clarinet key system. In the last quarter of the nineteenth century, Buffet introduced the full Boehm system, accepted worldwide and replaced the Albert System.

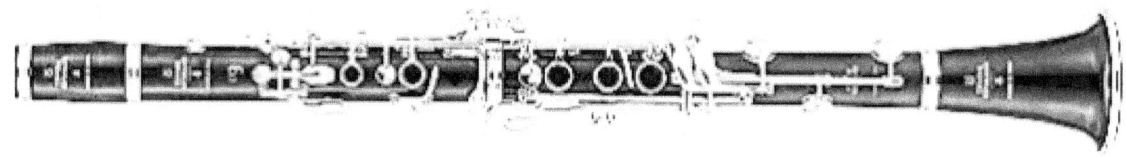

Boehm System Clarinet

Oskar Öhler (1858–1936) As clarinet technology developed to a point where a player could perform at a high level technically, a need grew to improve intonation and tone quality further. Öhler achieved this by repositioning the tone holes, modifying the fingering, and adding keys up to twenty-eight. He also reduced the diameter of the bore, extended its length, and decreased the diameter of the mouthpiece bore. Öhler's concepts for tone improvement were carried on by his students and eventually into the late twentieth century by the Wurlitzer Manufacturing Company, whose clarinets are most popular in Germany.

Öhler System Clarinet

The Saxophone

The Saxophone—The saxophone can be considered the first woodwind instrument invented instead of being an offshoot of some instrument from the past. Adolph Sax (1814–1894), born in Belgium, was a flutist, clarinetist, and instrument maker who received recognition for improving the timbre and key system and extending the lower range of the bass clarinet. He was also noted for making the ophicleide, a brass instrument played with a cup mouthpiece with tone holes fitted with as many as twelve woodwind-like padded keys. At one point, Sax reconstructed the ophicleide to be played with a clarinet mouthpiece.

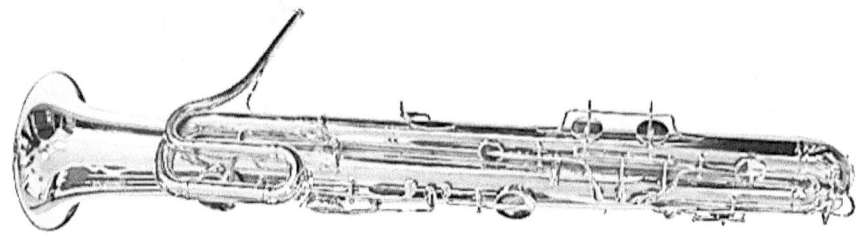

Ophicleide

With this background, we might guess that the stage was set in Sax's mind for a single reed woodwind instrument that would produce the sound characteristics of a brass instrument. Sax also intended to design an instrument to overblow at the octave rather than the twelfth, as does the clarinet to simplify the fingering. And so appeared the saxophone.

Sax designed and built a series of 14 saxophones spanning the tonal range from sopranino to contrabass. In 1846, he was granted a patent on these instruments, making him among the first instrument makers to purposely design, build, and produce a woodwind instrument rather than evolving from a series of previous such instruments.

After the patent expired, several other makers improved the saxophone, enhanced the key system to facilitate playing legato passages and chromatics, changed the bell, and extended the instrument's range to F6. Modifying the key work replaced two octave keys that operated the two octave vents with one key to control both vents.

The saxophone now holds an important position in all categories of instrumental music.

Below is a picture of the complete line of saxophones produced by the Selmer Musical Instrument Manufacturing Company. From left to right, they are the Eb Sopranino, Bb Soprano, Eb Alto, Bb Tenor, Eb Baritone, Bb Bass, and Eb Contrabass saxophones.

Saxophone Family Instruments

Saxophone Mouthpiece History

Progress in the study of the technology of musical instruments shows that an instrument's source of sound, namely the mouthpiece/reed, is primarily responsible for the quality of that sound. The mouthpiece is the major contributing factor to the quality of the tone produced. The saxophone's mouthpiece has proven to be an extreme example of this position. Saxophonists should select it carefully and consider their aptitude, physical characteristics, embouchure, and playing experience.

After reading this section, see pages 99-101 in the appendix at the end of this book to understand the different designs available and what each does to your sound production. Trial and error will lead you to the mouthpiece that best suits your sound production goal.

Many changes have taken place in the design of the saxophone's mouthpiece since the original was made in 1840. It has been lengthened, shortened, enlarged, made smaller, cored out, tapered, colored, and re-shaped using every sort of material conceivable. Each of these changes has contributed to the many opinions of the sound of the saxophone since each change in mouthpiece design resulted in a change in tone quality or timbre.

The early alto saxophone mouthpiece had a tube-shaped chamber/ throat with no taper. The throat was round, and the tone chamber had a bulbous portion preceding the window. The wall surfaces were concave, giving it a tone that was mellow and lacked the edge often associated with the saxophone.

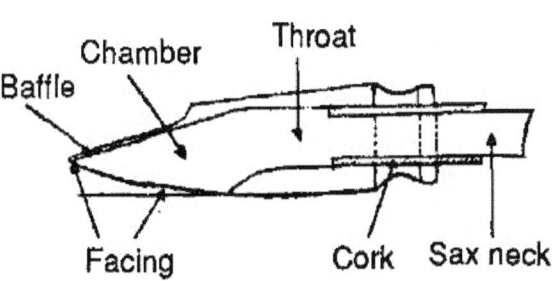

The 1930s saw the era of the large dance band, which demanded a sound that would be better matched with brass instruments. At that time, the woodwind and brass instruments were distributed equally in these bands. It became necessary to strengthen the sound of the saxophone to match that of the brasses.

Since sophisticated devices for sound evaluation were not yet available, those involved in research and development needed to rely on instinct to find remedies. They experimented with materials of various densities and expansion measurements and redesigned the structure of the mouthpiece interior. This experimentation produced many unsatisfactory mouthpieces that led to the decline of the reputation of the saxophone as a serious instrument.

During that time, one mouthpiece was developed, which modified the original and helped the saxophone regain some of its original popularity. The new model mouthpiece produced a richer tone, emphasizing the upper notes. Following that, the industry developed another design modeled on the shape of the clarinet mouthpiece. This mouthpiece produced an extraordinarily powerful and penetrating sound, and it gained favor from dance band music performers who competed with their brass-playing counterparts. Simultaneously, classical musicians stopped using the saxophone due to the instrument's increasing incompatibility with symphonic sounds.

Further experimentation with more advanced technological sound-evaluating devices led to smaller chambers, which proved unsatisfactory, and then to the double-tone chamber, which had a tapered cylindrical bore and a smaller tone chamber and throat. This mouthpiece produced a very aggressive sound, enabling a player to blast out the notes but creating a greater likelihood that the less experienced player might lose control of tone quality and intonation.

A mouthpiece that seemed to strike a suitable balance, including most of the above features, produced a tone acceptable to most "classical" musicians. Having a round chamber, it produced a smooth, mellow tone yet with a bright edge.

Double Reed Instruments

The Oboe

The Shawm—Dating back to the twelfth century, the Shawm was a double reed, conical bore instrument with eight tone holes, seven on the front and one on the back. The reed on some ancient shawms was surrounded by a windcap called a pirouette. With this device in place, the player's lips had no direct contact with the reed, making it possible to play the instrument while on horseback or marching.

As stated above, the disadvantage of this arrangement was the player's lack of control of intonation, expression, and nuanced volume normally afforded by direct contact with the reed. The resulting sound was piercing and very rich in overtones. Its strident tone was intended to compete with and accompany trumpets and percussion instruments.

As the Shawm evolved, the tone quality was somewhat modified by a change in the instrument's architecture. The range was increased by an octave, and the bore and tone holes were reduced in size. Various-sized shawms were made to cover the range from soprano to bass, the latter being less than successful due to its inconvenient size. The Shawm enjoyed popularity up to the middle of the seventeenth century when the oboe began to make its presence known.

The Oboe—The oboe is a derivative of the Shawm but with a more advanced key system that permits the player to perform with reasonable ease. Removing the windcap gives the player direct contact with the double reed, improving intonation, timbre, and volume control. The result is an instrument compatible with a modern orchestra instead of the Shawm, which produces a more "independent" sound.

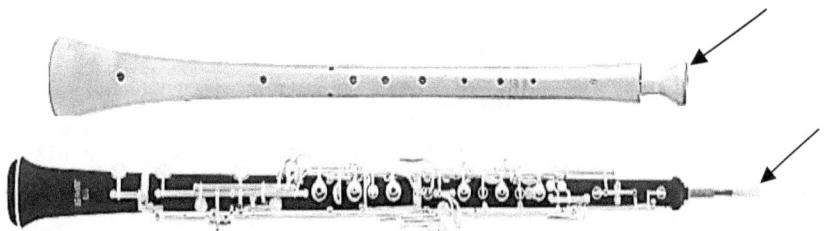

Shawm and Oboe

The oboe body was divided into three sections for convenient transportation and to facilitate repairs to the body. Damage to one section of a three-piece body is easier to deal with than damage to a one-piece body. A three-piece body can easily have a damaged section replaced without replacing the entire body.

In determining who invented the oboe, we can only guess based on word-of-mouth evidence from individuals in Europe's music world of the seventeenth-century era. Some historians credit Jean Hotteterre and Michel Danican Philidor as the inventors, separately or together.

The instrument known as the hautbois was a modification of the Shawm. The windcap was replaced by a double reed, and gradually, a key system evolved to accommodate the needs of the music. Four stages of development followed this. These were labeled Baroque, Classical, Viennese, and Conservatory models.

The original Baroque oboe was a simple instrument with three keys ranging from C4 to D6. To move to a higher register, the player had to increase the intensity of the air stream.

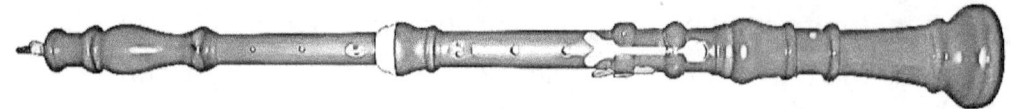

Baroque Oboe

During the classical period in music, a more advanced oboe was developed to satisfy the growing needs of the music performance community. The instrument had additional keys, a decreased bore diameter to ease playing in the upper register, and a vent key (not quite an octave key as we know it), which shifted up an octave more easily. It was later in the evolution that a true octave key was devised. The classical oboe range increased to F6.

Classical Oboe

The Viennese oboe began appearing in the last quarter of the nineteenth century. This is a hybrid of oboes from the Austrian/German system with a larger bore and a more complex key system. The upper register was also stronger in timbre and projection due to increased upper partials (see appendix on overtones). The larger bore, combined with wider and shorter reeds, produces a strong, double-reed sound with ease of playing. Note the differently shaped bell. The Viennese oboe might be considered the bridge from the antique to today's instrument.

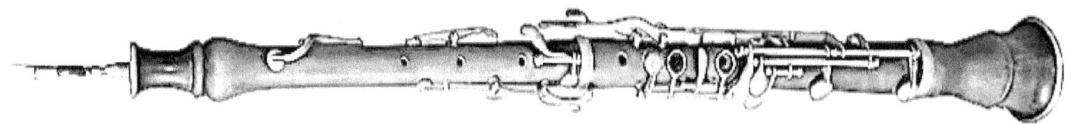

Early Viennese Oboe

The conservatory oboe was also developed at about the same time as the Viennese oboe and had a key system modeled after the Boehm oboe system. This system was not very popular but did act as the next step in developing the instrument to reach the point of the modern full conservatory system now in use. The full conservatory system has forty-five keys, some with rings and others with plateau keys. These oboes have a range from Bb3 to A6.

Conservatory Oboe

The modern oboe is the product of all that preceded it, with an excellent but complex key system and bore dimensions that produce the oboe sound we all recognize. This general design is now made in many different models to satisfy the entire range of notes used in music today.

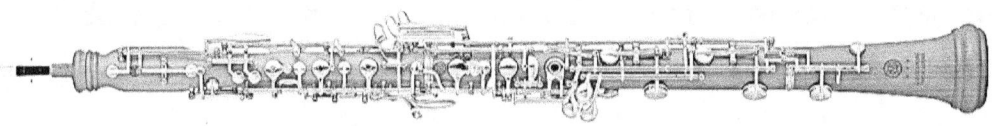

Modern Oboe

The Bassoon

The Bassoon—The Shawm, dulcian, and rankett are considered the forerunners of the bassoon. These instruments were popular for about two hundred years from the mid-sixteenth century. Like the bassoon, they used a double reed connected to a bocal. As the double reed shawm (described above) evolved into larger sizes, producing lower pitches, we could consider it the beginning of what would eventually become the bassoon.

The dulcian was a step closer to our current bassoon. Its bore was cone-shaped and long enough to be folded upon itself. However, unlike the bassoon, the dulcian was carved from one piece of maple.

The tone holes had to be drilled at an angle so that on the inside of the bore, they were placed according to the sound requirements, while on the outside of the instrument, they would fit a normal finger span of the player.

During the Dulcian period of popularity, eight different-sized versions were developed to complete the soprano to bass range. The instrument had eight tone holes and two keys. The dulcian continued to be popular as the bassoon began to make its appearance.

Dulcian

The rankett was also an instrument from the sixteenth century that may have added to the development of the bassoon in that the rankett was a double reed instrument with a range as low as G2.

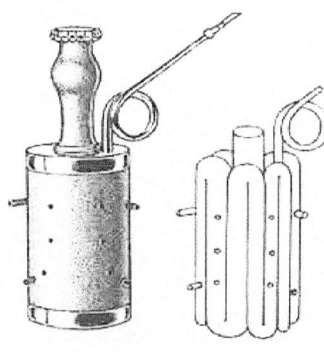

Rankett
(Complements of Wikipedia)

The unique difference was that rather than having a straight bore found in other woodwind instruments, the rankett was about five inches long but achieved the low range through a cylindrical bore within the body with nine tone holes spaced to accommodate the spread of a player's hand.

Other modifications in the tone holes and bore made by John Christian Denner mentioned above advanced the technology of the chalumeau to the point where he made the first extended-range baroque bassoon. He developed the rankett to the point where it was, in effect, a small bassoon.

Jacques Martin Hotteterre (1673–1763), also mentioned above, Jacques devised the oboe with a three-piece design with a separate head joint, body, and foot joint structure. In addition to being a prominent flutist, composer, and Renaissance man in the music world of his time, he is credited with being one of several individuals responsible for developing the bassoon.

As a member of a large family of instrument makers, we might guess that Hotteterre was able to use his musical ability, experience, and creativity in conjunction with the skills of his instrument-maker family members to develop and build an early bassoon. Hotteterre increased the bell's size, extended the bassoon's range, and designed the instrument in four sections so the bore could be more accurately machined.

Carl Almenraeder (1786–1846) designed a bassoon with 17 keys that could play a four-octave range chromatically. Almenraeder joined J.A. Heckel (1812–1877) in producing what would become the German Heckel system bassoon. Heckel went on to expand the bassoon range and create a contrabassoon. Both of these were prototypes for the bassoons used today.

The advancement of technology in musical instrument manufacturing and an increased understanding of the principles of acoustics enabled instrument makers to provide for the increased demands of the performing community. And so evolved the Heckle or German system and the Buffet or French system bassoons. These are two distinctly different designed instruments that, to date, serve two differing viewpoints on what a bassoon should be.

The Heckel (German) system features a complicated key system with up to 27 keys joined with a wider bore, producing a fuller sound. Heckel system bassoons currently enjoy popularity throughout most of the world, while the Buffet model has greater popularity in France, Spain, and Canada.

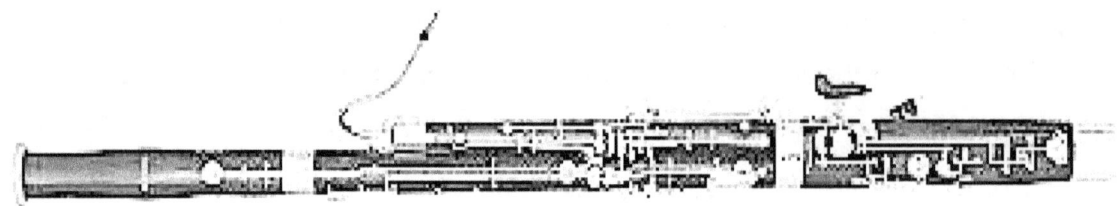

Heckel System Bassoon

The Buffet (French) design has a simple 22-key system joined with a narrow bore. The results are less complicated fingering requirements and more lyrical mellow tone quality.

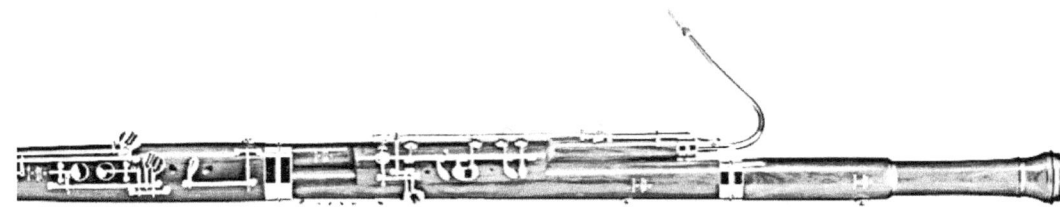

Buffet System Bassoon

Summary—The early history of woodwind instruments is, at best, vague and lacking in definitive structure. As far as we know, they began with the simple act of blowing air into some reed-like plant. Yet, they became more complex mechanically and acoustically than all the other instruments.

Because there is a shortage of documentation on the early phase of woodwind instrument history, it is necessary to guess their development. From Medieval times to the present, organologists (musical instrument scientists) have access to an almost overwhelming amount of documented history on how woodwind instruments began to be crafted and developed to the point at which we now enjoy their use.

The instruments of the woodwind family provide the music community with a listening pleasure that spans most of the notes with any emotion, from expressive lyricism to dynamic brilliance. These instruments can stand on their own as solo instruments, be part of a woodwind ensemble, or contribute to the sounds of any other combination of musical instruments. In a symphony orchestra, they are the core of the auditory transition between the string and brass sections.

From the primitive individuals who made the first sounds with a bamboo reed to the inventors, musicians, technicians, and visionaries who brought us up to the point where society is now fortunate enough to enjoy a listening experience that has become a precious possession of our music world, a profound thank you!

NOTES

Chapter 8

What Items (Accessories) Will I Need to Help Me Play My Saxophone?

To function properly, musical instruments require accessories. Three categories of accessories are available to enhance the playing experience: those that are necessary, those that make playing easier, and maintain an instrument, and those that are luxuries. The following accessories are needed to successfully play and maintain any of the instruments in the saxophone family. Because of the many brands of each product on the market, I will discuss this topic in general terms.

Lubricants—Saxophones have many moving parts which require regular lubrication. Searching for "saxophone key oil" in Google Images will show you various available products. The following is a description of different types of oils and their use.

In chapter 5, you learned how to decide how long an oil will work successfully before evaporating by rubbing a drop of oil between your thumb and index finger and judging how long the oil's oiling sensation lasts. Compare several oils against one another. Petroleum-based oils will probably last a shorter time than synthetic oils. The choice of oil is a very individual one.

Using Oil—The figure below shows key oil in a needle-type dispenser for easy distribution. The oils you use for each process will have to be your decision. Use the information to follow as a starting point to search the subject. The oils that are packaged with a needle applicator are very convenient.

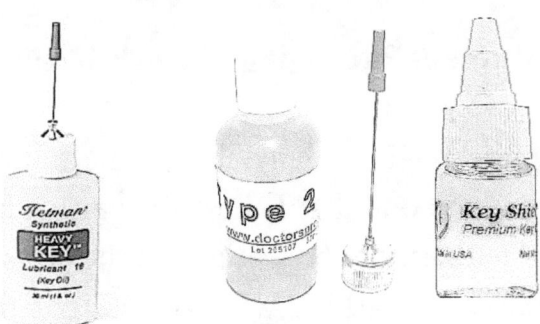

Key Oil Dispenser

Selecting Key Oil—There are many conflicting opinions on how often and with which oil is best. Some thoughts:

Light oil tends to evaporate more quickly than thicker oil.

Light oil is probably better if you are oiling frequently.

Light oil tends to travel down the post to the instrument's body. This is messy and will collect dust and lint and can get on the keypads.

To test the viscosity (thickness) of oil, start by shaking the bottle to see how the contents move. The slower the oil moves, the thicker it is.

To compare the thickness of several oils, place a drop of each, side by side, on one end of a smooth, flat surface. Then, raise that end of the surface and note the rate of speed at which the oils travel downward. Thicker oils will move more slowly.

With several choices, try each on one saxophone key using a different key for each trial. Do not combine different oils during the trial.

Cork Grease—Cork grease is used for the cork on your saxophone's neck. Many brands are available, each claiming its good quality above the others.

Different Packaging of Cork Grease

Saxophone Mouthpieces—The many saxophone mouthpieces on the market make it difficult to choose the one that is best for you. Additionally, no universal industry marking is used to describe the features of the parts of a mouthpiece. Most saxophone mouthpieces have a marking with the maker's name and some number indicators. Unfortunately, these numbers are privately owned, so a similar marking on two brands may mean different things.

For a beginner, it is best to start with the mouthpiece that comes with your instrument.

For more advanced players, here are some ideas that may help you choose. A good approach to beginning a search might be to review each part of the anatomy of a mouthpiece with attention to how it relates to your specific needs. The following is a repeat of chapter 2 for your convenience.

The facing (table) is the flat side where the reed is placed. It is the placement of the reed on the facing that produces the sound.

Facing can be short, medium, or long.

Longer facings favor lower sounds,

shorter facings favor higher sounds,

and medium facings strike a balance. Medium facing will probably be best for most students.

A professional marching band player's mouthpiece requirements are not likely to match those of a jazz or symphonic performer. The best you can do is try the mouthpiece to see how each satisfies your needs.

Centuries of trial and error have encouraged the industry to use glass, crystal, plastic, or hard rubber as the best substances. Although the material has some consequences, its importance must be judged with other design considerations in making a mouthpiece. See page 99 in the appendix for more on mouthpieces.

Mouthpiece Pouches—Saxophone mouthpiece pouches are available in various sizes and shapes. The interior structure is generally designed to protect the contents yet not to be instrument-specific. Most will hold any saxophone mouthpiece that will fit in the pouch. Below are three different kinds of mouthpiece pouches. The choice is personal.

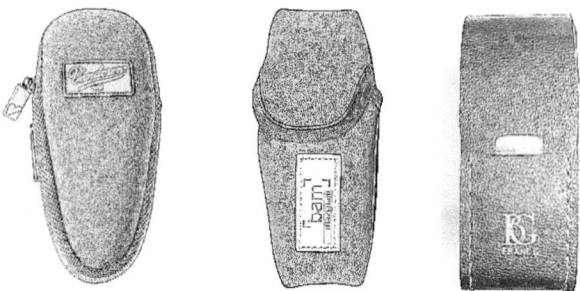

Mouthpiece Pouches

Cleaning Brushes—Saxophone mouthpieces and key cleaning brushes are available in a variety of shapes and sizes suited for every possible use. The figure below illustrates some of these brushes and a complete saxophone cleaning kit. There are many more. Your choice should be the products that will satisfy your needs.

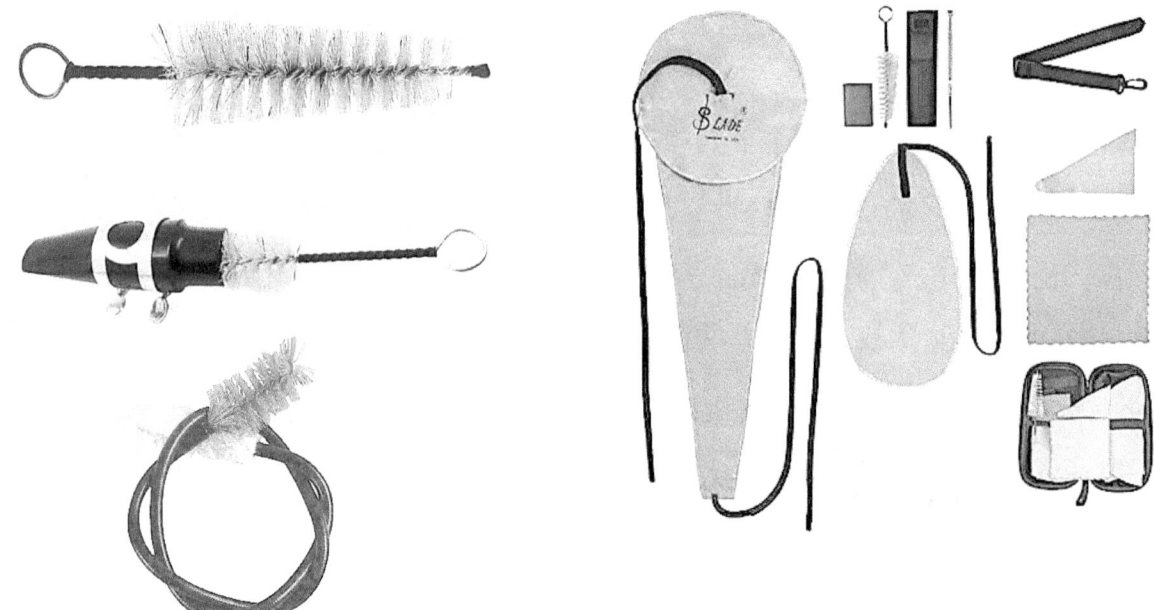

Saxophone Cleaning Equipment

Tuning Forks—Invented in 1711 by John Shore, the tuning fork is the most basic device designed to determine pitch accurately. The device consists of a U-shaped metal form with a handle at the base of the U.

Holding the tuning fork by the handle, when the tines (prongs) are struck on a hard surface, they are set into a vibrating pattern, which produces a tone.

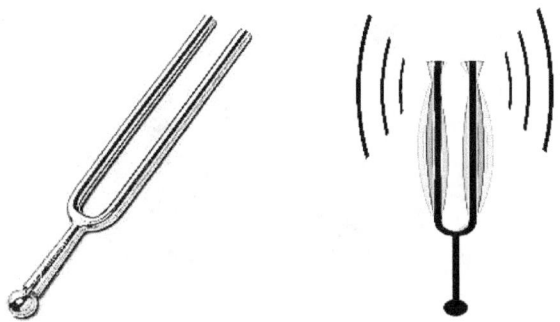

Tuning Fork and One with Vibrating Tines

Pitch Pipes—A chromatic pitch pipe is round and contains a marked opening for every pitch in the chromatic scale. The notes start at C and progress chromatically up an octave to the next C in the scale. You can choose any note, slide the white marker to that note's position on the pitch pipe, blow into that hole, and hear the pitch selected.

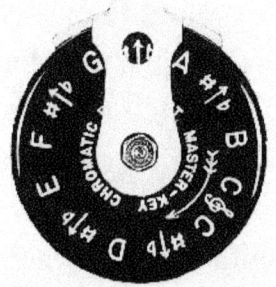

Chromatic Pitch Pipe

Electronic Tuners—Below are pictured three kinds of electronic tuners. One type offers a three-in-one calibrator, tuner, and metronome, and the other two are clip-one, showing a big LED display of the pitches you are tuning. When you play a note, the screen will show if the sound is sharp, flat, or spot-on. You can adjust the saxophone or your embouchure until the correct pitch is reached.

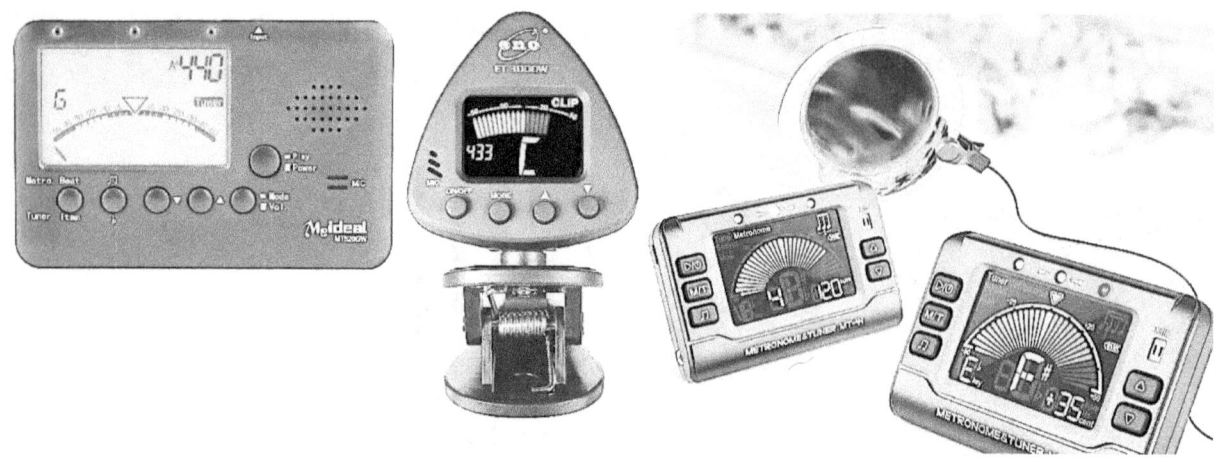

Electronic Tuners

    Apps or Applications—Aids to tuning appear on websites, iPads, cell Phones, and the Internet. Use them wisely, but try to avoid being distracted by the charm of technology.

    Summary of Tuners—In this writing, Amazon.com shows five pages, each with about fifteen different tuners for a total of seventy-five tuners of all kinds now on the market. The choices start with a simple, inexpensive device with tuned pipes that you can blow to produce the desired pitch to match. The advantage of this product is that it requires you to listen to and think of pitch instead of relying on visual aids to tune. Music is a hearing art, so every act that will help train your ear to hear and your mind to think of sound is another step toward success.

    Electric Pickups—Amplified saxophones share the same basic sound equipment as electric guitars. These include pickups, pre-amplifiers, amplifiers, equalizers, and speakers.

    Acoustic Electric Saxophones—An amplified saxophone is a traditional instrument to which a pickup is added.

    Two kinds of pickups in general use are the magnetic pickup, which is built into parts of an instrument's body, and a microphone in different locations depending on the instrument. The pickups are connected with a cable to an amplifier using the same equipment mentioned above that is used for the electric guitar. With the proper equipment, they can also be wireless.

The condenser microphone is most popular because of its low cost and true sound. This microphone converts sound waves into electrical energy, sends them to an amplifier, and sends them to a speaker. A condenser microphone can easily be clipped onto almost any instrument, and you have an amplified (electric) instrument.

The downside to this microphone is that while it will pick up the saxophone's sound, it will also pick up surrounding sounds caused by handling the instrument, such as bumps, knocks, and sometimes even the action of the keys in motion. There is also a danger of feedback when using this type of microphone.

Clip-On Condenser Microphone

Another condenser microphone is the piezoelectric microphone, which receives vibrations through direct contact with the instrument. This type of pickup is best placed on the neck of a saxophone, where it will pick up the total quality of the sound.

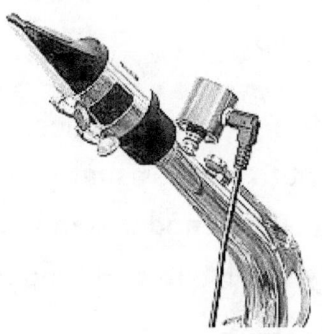

Direct Contact Pickup

Another pickup type is a battery-operated clip-on wireless microphone that transmits the signal wirelessly. This unit has a noise reduction chip that will filter out surrounding noise.

Battery Operated Clip-On Pickup

Music Stands—Correct posture and playing position are essential to successful performance on any instrument. A music stand is a very important aid in keeping that posture.

Music stands are sold in three basic designs. Some stands fold, others are rigid or non-folding, and there are tabletop versions.

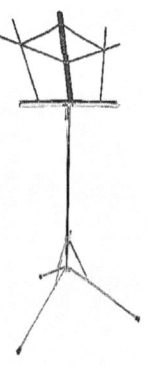

The folding or sheet music stand is very useful for a beginning student. It is lightweight, totally portable, and very inexpensive. Folding stands can also be purchased with a carrying case for more convenient portability. These stands can easily be knocked over, and the lightweight parts can be bent out of shape.

The rigid design stand, sometimes called a concert, stage, or orchestra music stand, is not convenient to carry, usually quite heavy, and is intended to be used in one place. This model stand is more expensive than the folding stand but is very stable, able to hold a good amount of music, and is practically indestructible.

A tabletop stand is small, very portable, does not have legs, and is lightweight and inexpensive. It can be placed on any stable surface for complete flexibility. The problem is that should it be on a tabletop, the music could be too low for you to see while standing and keeping a proper playing position. This stand is best used if you use it while sitting. A folding, decorative, and concert tabletop stand is pictured below.

Tabletop Stands

Swabs—Swabs are essential for the care of any saxophone. The figure below shows a pull-through swab, one with a brush interior, a pad saver, and a neck swab.

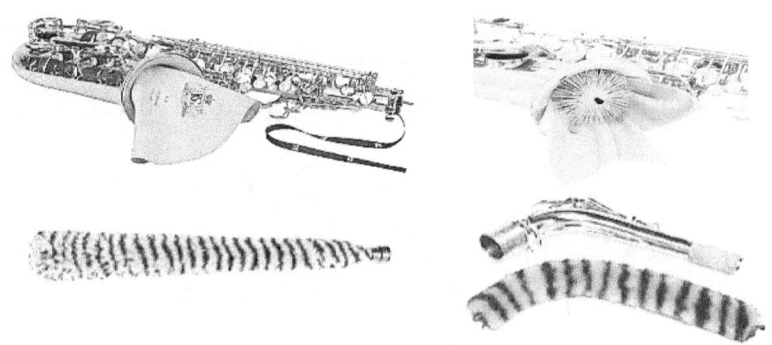

Swabs

Straps—Straps help you hold your saxophone during long playing sessions. The figure below shows three different kinds of saxophone straps. From left to right, there is a traditional design, a padded model, and a harness. There are many more.

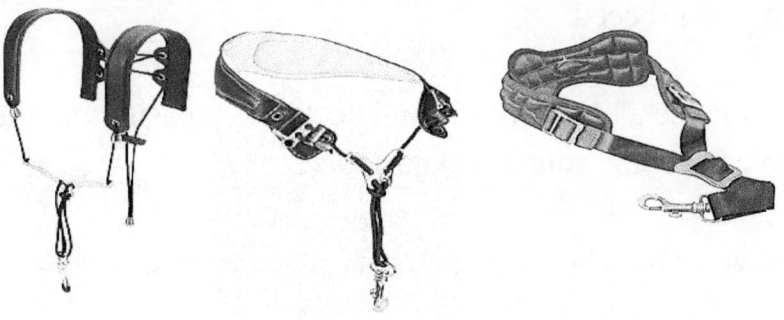

Saxophone Neck Straps

Thumb and Finger Rests—These products are designed to relieve the pressure on your thumb while holding a saxophone. Below are a thumb rest pad, a thumb cushion, and palm key finger protectors. There are many more.

  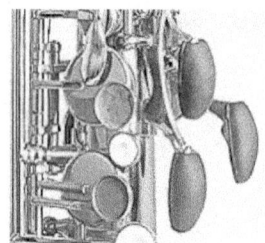

Thumb and Finger Rests

Reeds—Reeds are the source of sound on saxophones. Better reeds produce better sounds, so learning as much as possible about reeds is valuable.

The two major types of reeds now on the market are those made of cane called Arundo Donax, a distant relative of bamboo, and those made of various synthetic materials.

Reeds are categorized by thickness with numbers 1 through 5 in half-number units. You will find reeds in sizes marked 1, 1.5, 2, 2.5, 3, 3.5, etc., up to the number 5. The softest will be 1, and the hardest will be 5. These numbered classifications are not the same throughout the industry, so a number 2.5 reed by one manufacturer may not be the same strength as that of another manufacturer using the same number.

When buying reeds, the first step is to choose from famous makers. Don't rely on the maker's claims. Ask everyone you know who uses the reeds you are interested in, their opinion, and proceed.

Softer reeds produce a brighter tone and do so more easily, but they may be a bit more difficult to control the sound they produce.

A harder reed will give a bolder sound but can have difficulty playing in the lower register. However, it is better in the high register.

Cane reeds should be some shade of medium to dark yellow. This shows that the wood has been properly cured and is ready for use. Do not buy green reeds.

Because the upper part of a reed is translucent, you can hold it up to a light and see its inner structure. It is best if the vertical fibers are evenly spaced, parallel, and have an even color.

Reed Fibers

There are different styles of cutting a saxophone reed. In the figure below, the reed on the left has a "U" shaped cut where the taper begins. This is called the American cut. The reed on the right, a French cut, has a section of cane removed horizontally in place of the "U."

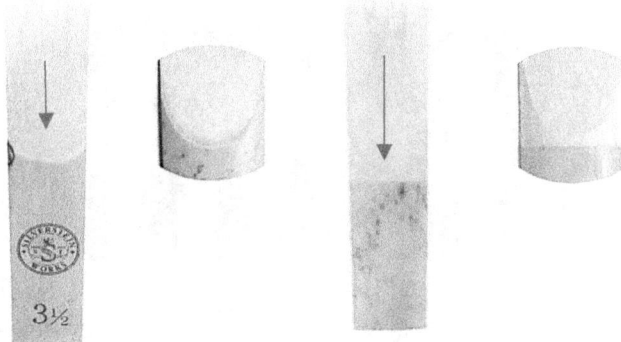

American and French Cut Reeds

American cut reeds can have a thicker tip with less material in the heart. The result is a fuller, more controlled sound.

The French cut is the opposite, with a thicker heart and a thinner tip, giving the player increased suppleness with a quicker response.

There are mouthpiece facings (lays) to match these two reed cuts. The American cut mouthpiece tends toward a flatter lay that will respond better with the American cut reed. The French mouthpiece has an increased curve to the lay, requiring a French cut reed.

The figure below is a cutout view of a saxophone mouthpiece showing the reed's relationship to the facing.

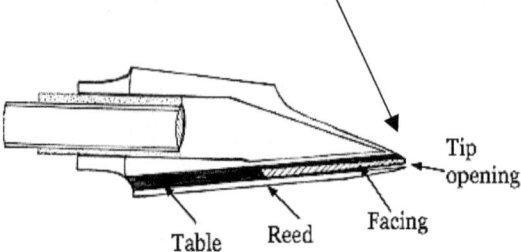

Saxophone Mouthpiece Sections

Plastic Reeds—Plastic reeds copy the natural fibers of a cane reed with artificial fibers made of synthetic polymers. These reeds look, feel, and, in the opinion of many, sound like traditional cane reeds. Plastic reeds are durable, consistent in their structure, reliable in their sound production, and have a long lifespan. The figure below shows just a few plastic reeds on the market.

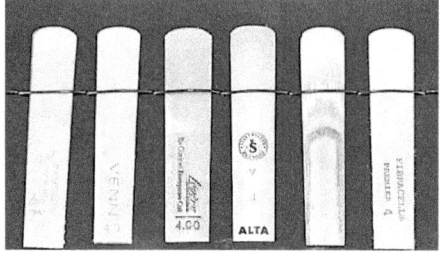

Plastic Reeds

Reed Cases—Reed cases pay for themselves by preventing reeds from being damaged in transit or storage. The figure below shows single reed cases, another for several reeds, and one with a humidifier to prevent reeds from drying out.

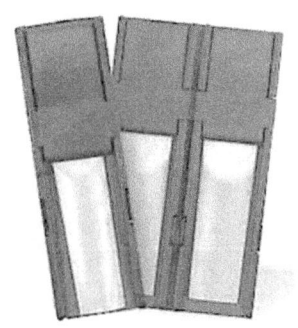 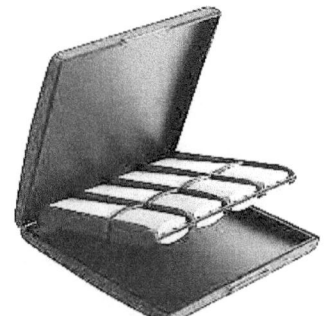 

Reed Cases

Saxophone Screwdrivers—The screws used on saxophone key mechanisms have very small, slotted heads. Use the correct size screwdriver to turn or remove one of these screws. A screwdriver with a head that is a bit too small but does fit in the screw slot may allow the screwdriver to slip out of the screw slot and possibly strip the screw head.

The figure below shows two sets of screwdrivers suited to working with most saxophone key systems. Remember, when in doubt, do not force the screw if it does not respond immediately. Bring the instrument to a professional.

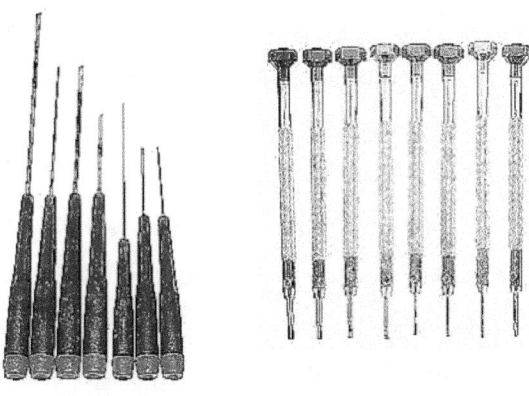

Woodwind Key Screwdrivers

Ligatures—Ligatures are designed to hold a reed onto a mouthpiece. Original ligatures were made of various types of cord that tied the reed to the mouthpiece. Over the years, a series of theories developed on the effect of a ligature on tone quality and reed response. As a result, you have numerous choices to select the one that is best for you. Some are illustrated below.

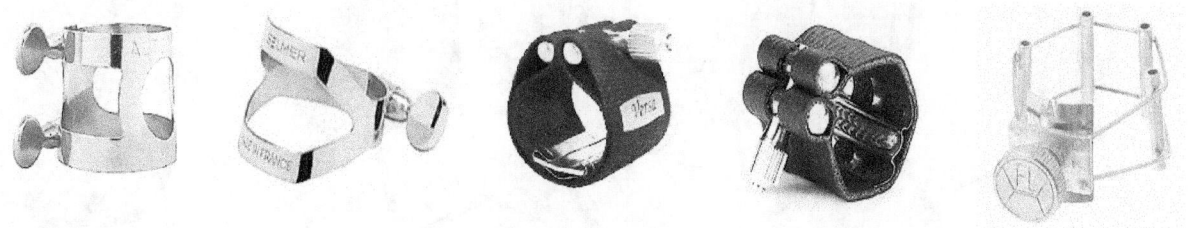

Saxophone Ligatures

Lyres—A lyre is a portable music stand. It can be attached to an instrument and goes wherever the instrument goes. Lyres are used to hold the music for marching band instruments. The figure below shows a traditional lyre and a "MobileLyr," which displays music from your mobile phone.

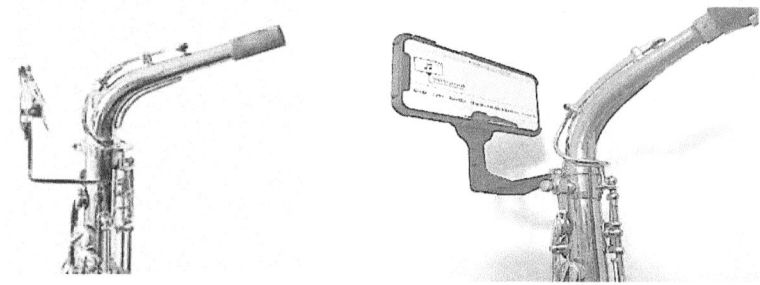

Saxophone Lyres

Instrument Stands—There is a stand designed to safely hold every saxophone when not in use. Since there are so many different stands, it is best to search "saxophone stands" on Google Images and scroll down to see the wide variety available.

Click on the picture of the one you like best, then click on the "visit page" for additional information on the product. When you find something interesting, your best move might be to order it online if the return policy is favorable.

If you prefer to shop directly, print the desired product page and begin the search at your local music store. Below is pictured a single saxophone, tenor/soprano/alto, tenor/clarinet/alto, and alto/flute stands. There are many more combinations.

Instrument Stands

Saxophone Cases—Cases are available in hard and soft models. Soft cases are often called "gig bags." If padded, they will provide sufficient protection for normal use. A hard case is best if the instrument is to travel or be transported by young players. Below are three examples of saxophone gig bags.

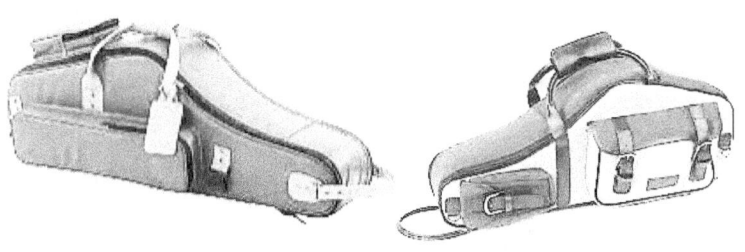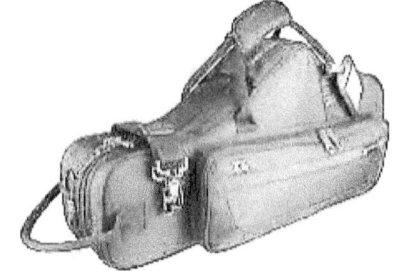

Soft Saxophone Cases

Hard cases are heavier than soft cases but offer greater protection for the instrument. Some hard cases are made of wood and covered with various durable fabrics. The inner linings are shaped to fit the instrument, padded, and often lined with velour. A simpler and usually less expensive construction for a hard case is lightweight and durable molded plastic with an inner lining of soft padding with plush fabric. The figures below show two of the many hard saxophone cases in use.

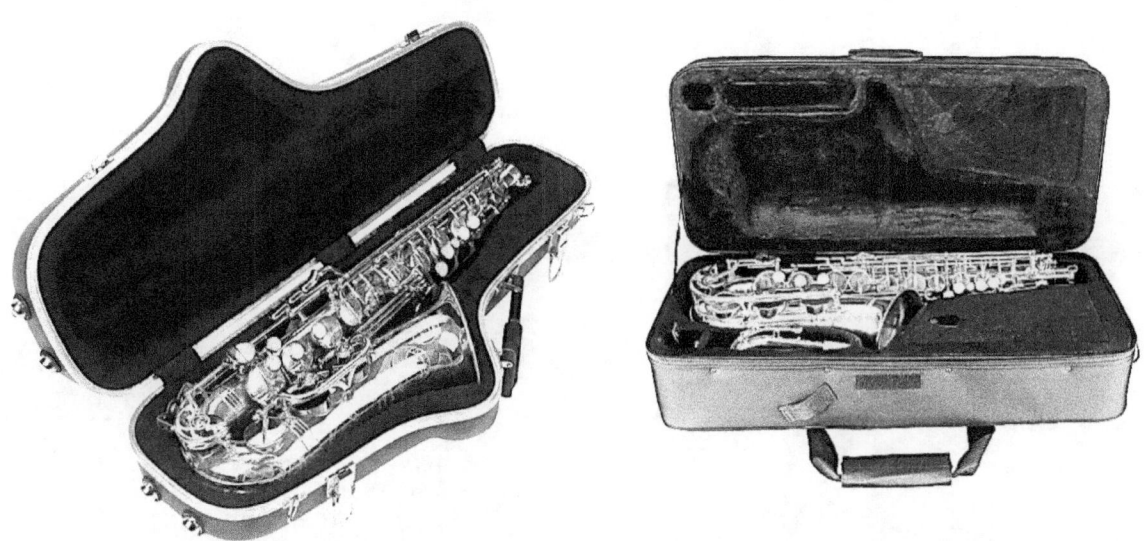

Hard Saxophone Cases

Summary—The introduction to this chapter states that musical instrument accessories fall into the categories of those that are necessary, those that make playing more enjoyable, and those that are luxuries. These three categories are not divided by strict rules. What may be one person's luxury could well be considered by another to be a necessity. As is usually the case in music, the decision is unique to the individual. The examples in this chapter sample what is available in each category. There are, in fact, hundreds of additional variations on the market.

Appendix

Note: In this appendix, you will learn words used in the study of the science of sound. When these words appear, they will be followed by the more common term in parentheses.

Scientific Pitch Notation—The following explains a system used throughout music study called *Scientific Pitch Notation*. This is a valuable tool that can serve you throughout your music career.

Scientific Pitch Notation helps you know exactly where a note is located on the staff without seeing the note in print. This system uses alphanumerics (a combination of letters and numerals) to tell you exactly where a note is in the entire range of notes. An example would be middle C, whose alphanumeric name is C4. The C one octave below middle C is C3. The C an octave above middle C is C5. The notes going up between these Cs keep the C's numeral until the next C is reached. Examples would be C4, D4, E4, F4, G4, A4, B4, C5, D5, etc. The figure below shows the alphanumeric symbol for all notes.

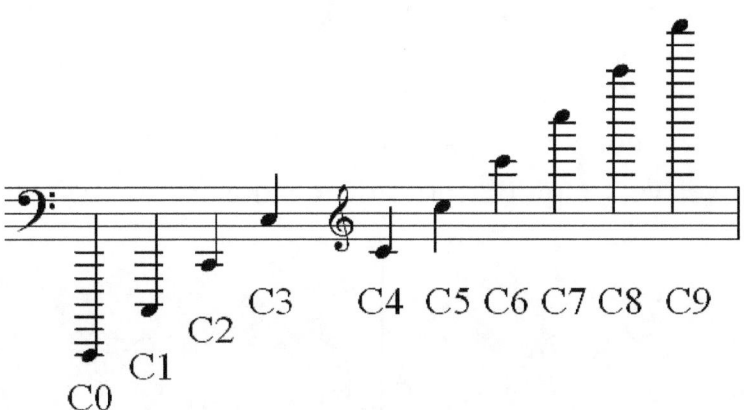

Scientific Pitch Notation

Sound—Sound occurs when something causes vibrations in the air. The vibrations travel by waves of air pushed against one another, acting as a train would when the last car is pushed, and each car moves in front of the last one. This is called a chain reaction.

Molecules (tiny bits) of air push against one another to make sound travel. The grouping of tight molecules pictured below is named compression. The more open pattern is called rarefaction.

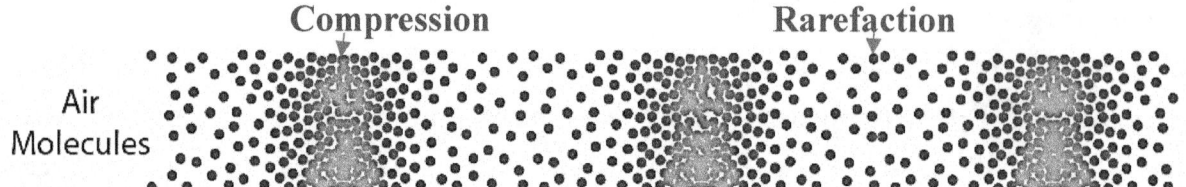

The combined action of compression and rarefaction results in a complete cycle of sound.

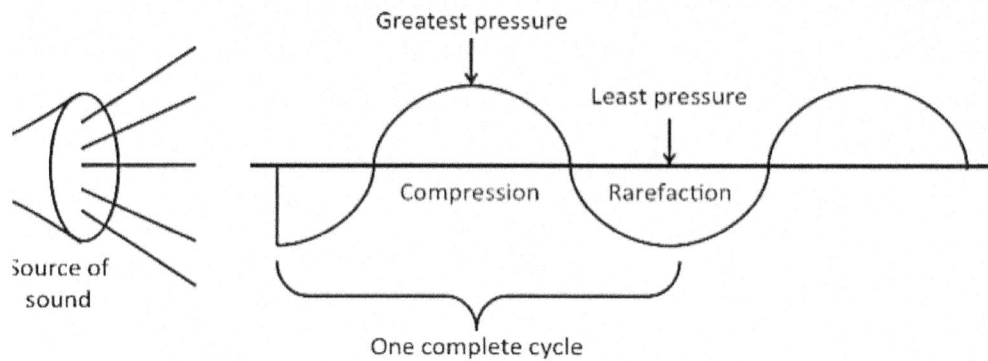

Vibration—If you look very closely at a guitar string that has been plucked, you will see that it moves very rapidly from side to side.

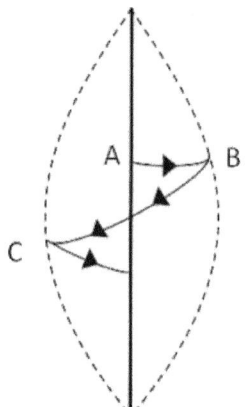

It moves from the center (A) to one side (B) and back across the center (A) to the other side (C). This entire voyage completes *one cycle*.

Cycles per Second (cps) or Hertz (Hz) named after the physicist Heinrich Hertz, refers to the number of complete cycles per second, so 30 Hz means 30 cycles per second. Any tone results from the number of vibrations or cycles per second. "A" 440 is the tone produced by an instrument producing 440 vibrations or cycles per second. Below are some examples of notes with their cps.

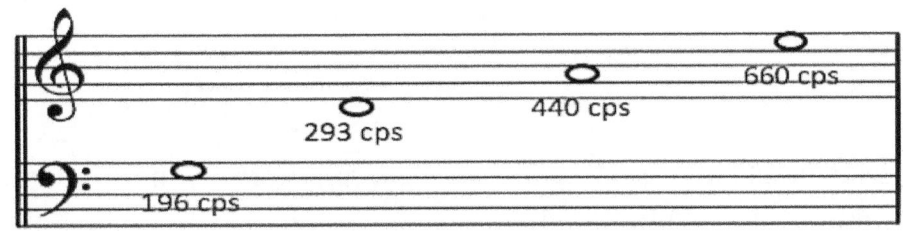

Cycles per Second

Sine Wave—When sound is created on a musical instrument, it produces a pattern of vibrations. These vibrations include a fundamental (basic) pitch and several other related pitches with less amplitude (volume). The fundamental pitch alone is a *pure tone* and can be pictured as a simple wave.

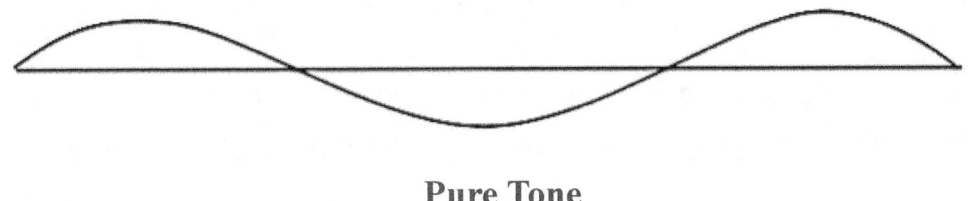

Pure Tone

Amplitude—Amplitude refers to the volume or loudness of a sound. Greater amplitude produces louder sounds. Less amplitude produces softer sounds.

Harmonics—When a pure tone is produced on a saxophone, it is joined by a series of related sounds or tones called harmonics. Other terms used for harmonics are overtones or upper partials. Any of these three terms can be used.

Harmonics (overtones or upper partials) are less important vibrations sounding with the fundamental (basic pitch) but with less amplitude (volume).

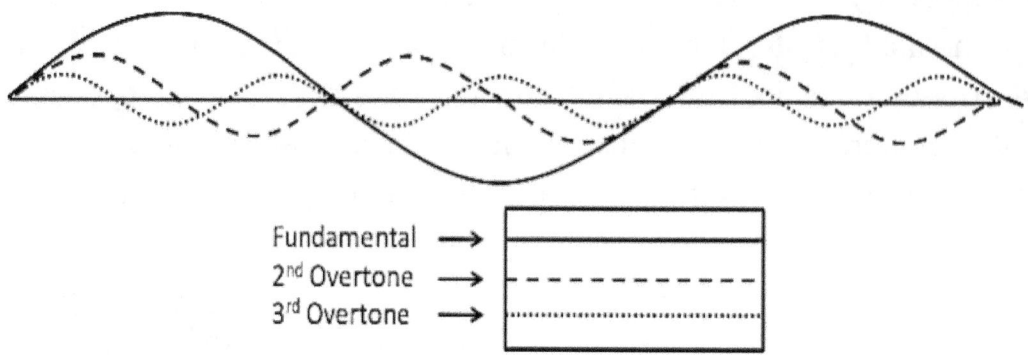

Harmonics cannot be heard as notes but are additions to the fundamental (basic pitch). Combining a basic pitch with harmonics results in timbre (sound Quality).

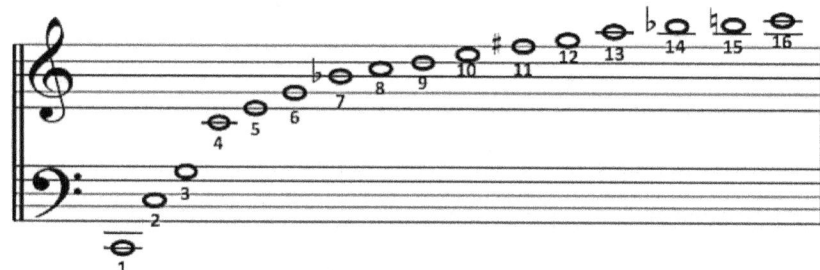

Harmonic Sequence

Timbre—Timbre is the product of adding tones to a fundamental pitch. These additional sounds, referred to as harmonics (overtones or upper partials), result from the built-in sound features of the instrument producing the sound. For note C, these sounds follow the harmonic sequence pictured above and are present in most tones. The same interval pattern would occur for any note.

The difference in timbre results from the amplitude of the harmonics and how they relate in volume to the fundamental pitch. Stronger harmonics produce a timbre of greater intensity. Less amplitude of the harmonics will produce a less intense timbre. Tones played on the oboe have strong harmonics, producing a tone that can be identified as having an intense timbre. On the other hand, the flute has a comparatively weak set of harmonics and produces a more mellow tone.

Tone—Tone is a combination of pitch, volume, and timbre (the special quality of a pitch).

Pitch is the highness or lowness of a tone. The notes of an ascending scale (do, re, mi, fa, sol, la, ti, do) go up in pitch or are successively higher. The notes go down in pitch or are successively lower in a descending scale (do, ti, la, sol, fa, mi, re, do).

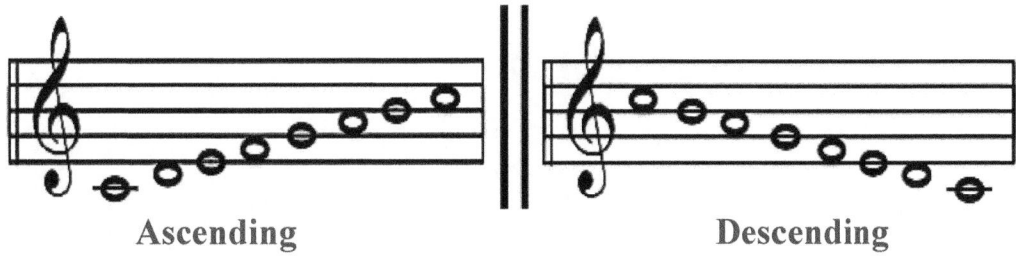

Ascending **Descending**

Any series of notes can take one of only three possible directions in pitch. They can ascend (A), descend (B), or remain the same (C).

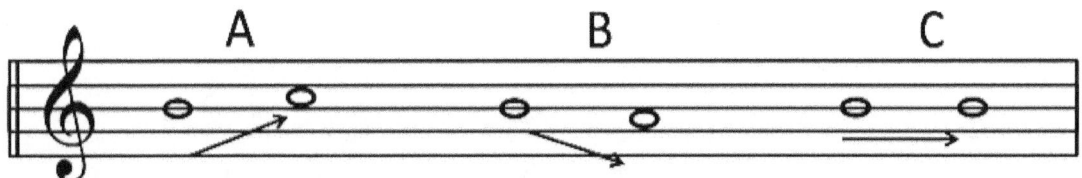

Summary—As you study your instrument, you are learning how to read music. Use that information to work the mechanics of your saxophone to produce sounds, and then, using your artistic sense, turn those sounds into music. A terrific achievement. However, there is an underlying study that is not usually given much attention. That is the study of sound.

The chapter you just read gives you a very slight overview of some of the many topics in that subject. You learned words like scientific pitch notation, vibrations, compression, rarefaction, cycles per second, tone, amplitude, and harmonics. Those are just a few topics that are in the study of sound.

As you progress in your saxophone studies, include some of these sound topics, and you will be able to apply that knowledge to your music performance and be a better, more knowledgeable musician.

NOTES

Glossary of Woodwind Instrument Terms

Adjustment Screws—a screw used to adjust key systems.

Alphasax—a redesigned saxophone for smaller players.

Annealing—applying heat to brass to change its shape.

Aulos—an ancient Greek flute-like instrument found in Greek art.

Baffle—the lower part of the reed side of a single reed mouthpiece.

Baroque—a decorative performance style or any art form practiced during the seventeenth and eighteenth centuries.

Barrel—the first section of a clarinet after the mouthpiece.

Bass Joint—the bassoon section located between the boot and bell joints.

Bell—the lowest section of a saxophone, clarinet, oboe, or bassoon.

Bell Joint—the last section of a bassoon.

Billet—a section of wood in the first stages of woodwind construction.

Boot Joint—the second and lowest section of a bassoon body.

Bore—the inner tube of a musical instrument in which the vibrating column of air becomes a tone.

Chalumeau—the precursor to the clarinet and the name of its lowest range.

Clarinet—a category of single reed cylindrical bore woodwind instruments.

Clarineo Lyons C Clarinet—A lightweight model of the Bb clarinet designed for young students.

Classical Music—Music composed during the eighteenth through the nineteenth century.

Closed Hole—a woodwind instrument key with a pad covering a tone hole.

Conservatory System—the key system on an oboe.

Contrabassoon—a lower-pitched version of a bassoon.

Cork Pads—pads made of cork used on woodwind instrument keys.

Crown—the first section of a flute head joint.

Crumhorn—a double reed woodwind windcap instrument from the Renaissance period.

Double Reed—a two-bladed reed used without a mouthpiece on instruments in the oboe and bassoon families.

Ebonite—a manmade hard rubber product used to make woodwind instrument bodies.

Facing—the upper segment of the reed side of a saxophone mouthpiece.

Finger—(see paddle) the section of a woodwind key where the player's finger is applied.

Fingering—the pattern used on the keys of a woodwind instrument to play a note.

Fish Skin Pads—woodwind instrument pads with fish skin used to cover their contact surface.

Flat Shelf—the edge shelf section of a flute head joint embouchure hole.

Flat Spring—one of three types of springs used to return a key to its rest position.

Fulcrum—the pivot point on a woodwind instrument key.

Fundamental—the basic pitch upon which overtones are built.

Grenadilla—a close-grained, dark-colored, dense wood used to make woodwind instrument bodies.

Harmonics—pitches related to a fundamental pitch but sounding in lesser degrees of volume.

Head Joint— the first section of a flute. A head joint has an embouchure hole into which the player blows air to produce a sound.

Intonation—the degree of accuracy with which a pitch is produced. A note can be in tune, sharp, or flat.

Key Pad Cup—the part of a woodwind key into which a pad is placed to cover a tone hole.

Key Springs—springs made of wire, blue steel, or other alloys installed to return a woodwind key to its original point of rest.

Key System—an arrangement of keys on a woodwind instrument.

Kinder Klari—a small E-flat clarinet modified to ease use by small hands.

Lay—(facing) the upper section of the reed side of a saxophone mouthpiece.

Leather Pads—leather in place of fish skin used to surface the contact side of a woodwind instrument keypad.

Ligature—a band of metal or other material used to hold a reed on a saxophone mouthpiece.

Lower Joint—the lower section of the body of a clarinet or oboe.

Mouthpiece—the first part of a woodwind instrument into which the player will blow to produce sound.

Neck—the uppermost section of a saxophone onto which the mouthpiece is connected.

Oboe—a double reed woodwind instrument with a range of about two octaves producing tones strong in upper partials.

Open Hole—a woodwind instrument key with a cup with a hole in its center.

Pad—a soft, fish skin or leather padded disc in woodwind instrument key pad cups that make contact with and seal tone holes.

Paddle—the part of a woodwind key that the player's finger contacts.

Pitch—the highness or lowness of a tone.

Plateau Keys—see closed hole.

Posts—knob-like elements holding the keys onto the body of a woodwind instrument.

Professional Level—the highest quality musical instrument.

Reed—a formed strip of cane used as a sound generator on woodwind instruments.

Resonator—a hard surfaced disc added to the center of a keypad to increase the resonance of a woodwind instrument.

Resonite—acrylonitrile butadiene styrene (ABS) used to make bodies for inexpensive woodwind instruments.

Rib Construction—a strip of metal used to reinforce posts on flutes and saxophones.

Rosewood—a beautifully grained lighter, colored wood used to make clarinet and oboe bodies.

Saxonette—a clarinet-like instrument with a neck and upturned bell used as a transitional instrument between the clarinet and saxophone.

Saxophone—a single reed, brass-bodied woodwind instrument with padded keys.

Scientific Pitch Notation—an alphanumeric system combining letters and numbers to identify the location of a note on the staff.

Shawm—a double reed, wind-capped predecessor to the oboe, popular in the Medieval and Renaissance periods.

Side Rails—the two narrow sides of a saxophone mouthpiece bore.

Silicon Pads—a durable pad with a silicon surface used on woodwind instruments.

Single-Reed Mouthpiece—a mouthpiece designed to use a single reed, typically for a clarinet or saxophone.

Sonic Welding—high-frequency sound waves used to install posts on plastic instrument bodies.

Sound Production—the process unique to each instrument used to generate sound.

Spatula—the fingered part of a woodwind instrument key.

Spring—strips of various metal alloys used to return a woodwind instrument key to its rest position.

Staple—the cork-covered tubular bottom of a double reed inserted into an instrument.

Step-Up (Intermediate)—the next step up in quality and workmanship from a student-level musical instrument.

Student-Level—the least expensive entry-level musical instrument.

Tenon—the projection that joins each section of a woodwind instrument.

Throat—the inner section of a saxophone mouthpiece between the chamber and the bore.

Tip Rail—the rounded top edge of the window of a saxophone mouthpiece.

Tone Holes—holes used to change pitches in the body of a woodwind instrument.

Transposition—changing any combination of notes to a different key.

Triple Reed—a reed with three blades.

Tuning—the act of adjusting the pitch of an instrument.

Upper Joint—the upper section of the body of a clarinet or oboe.

Windcap—a cylinder that encloses a double reed.

Window—the opening between the rails of a saxophone mouthpiece.

Wing Joint—the first section of a bassoon's body after the bocal.

Zummara—a two-bodied nineteenth-century mid-eastern woodwind instrument.

NOTES

Dictionary of Saxophone Terms

For your convenience, this dictionary is a review of saxophone-only terms from the woodwind glossary above.

Adjustment Screws—a screw that facilitates key adjustments to close tolerance.

Alphasax—a redesigned saxophone for smaller players.

Annealing—applying heat to brass to change its molecular structure.

Baffle—the lower part of the reed side of a saxophone mouthpiece.

Baroque—a decorative performance style or any art form practiced during the seventeenth and eighteenth centuries.

Bell—the lowest section of a saxophone.

Bore—the inner tube of a wind instrument in which the vibrating column of air becomes a tone.

Facing—the upper segment of the reed side of a saxophone mouthpiece.

Finger—the section of a woodwind key where the player's finger is applied.

Fingering—the pattern used on the keys of a saxophone to play a note.

Fish Skin Pads—fish skin used to cover the contact surface of some woodwind instrument pads.

Flat Spring—one of three types of springs used to return a key to its rest position.

Fulcrum—the pivot point on a saxophone key.

Fundamental—the basic pitch upon which overtones are built.

Harmonics—pitches related to a fundamental pitch but sounding in lesser degrees of amplitude or volume.

Intonation—the degree of accuracy with which a pitch is produced. A note can be in tune, sharp, or flat.

Key Pad Cup—the part of a woodwind key into which a pad is placed to cover a tone hole.

Key Springs—springs made of wire, blue steel, or other alloys installed to return a woodwind key to its original point of rest.

Key System—an arrangement of keys on a saxophone.

Lay—(facing) the upper section of the reed side of a saxophone mouthpiece.

Leather Pads—leather in place of fish skin used to surface the contact side of a saxophone keypad.

Ligature—a band of metal or other material used to hold a reed on a saxophone mouthpiece.

Mouthpiece—the first part of a saxophone into which the player will blow to produce sound.

Neck—the uppermost section of a saxophone onto which the mouthpiece is connected.

Pad—a soft, fish skin or leather padded disc in saxophone key pad cups that make contact with and seal tone holes.

Paddle—the part of a woodwind key that the player's finger contacts.

Pitch—the highness or lowness of a tone.

Posts—knob-like elements holding the keys onto the body of a saxophone.

Professional level—the highest quality musical instrument.

Reed—a formed strip of cane used as a sound generator on saxophones.

Resonator—a hard surfaced disc added to the center of a keypad to increase the resonance of a saxophone.

Rib Construction—a strip of metal used to reinforce posts on flutes and saxophones.

Saxonette—a saxophone-like instrument with a neck and upturned bell used as a transitional instrument between the clarinet and saxophone.

Saxophone—a single reed, brass-bodied woodwind instrument with padded keys.

Scientific Pitch Notation—an alphanumeric system combining letters and numbers to identify the location of a note on the staff.

Side Rails—the two narrow sides of a saxophone mouthpiece bore.

Silicon Pads—a durable pad with a silicon surface used on saxophones.

Single-Reed Mouthpiece—A mouthpiece that uses a single reed, typically for a clarinet or saxophone.

Sonic Welding—high-frequency sound waves used to install posts on plastic instrument bodies.

Sound Production—the process unique to each instrument used to generate sound.

Spatula—the fingered part of a saxophone key.

Spring—strips of various metal alloys used to return a saxophone key to its rest position.

Step-Up (Intermediate)—the next step up in quality and workmanship from a student-level musical instrument.

Student-Level—the least expensive entry-level musical instrument.

Tenon—the projection that joins the neck to a saxophone.

Throat—the inner section of a saxophone mouthpiece between the chamber and the bore.

Tip Rail—the rounded top edge of the window of a saxophone mouthpiece.

Tone Holes—holes used to change pitches in the body of a saxophone.

Transposition—changing any combination of notes to a different key.

Tuning—the act of adjusting the pitch of an instrument.

Window—the opening between the rails of a saxophone mouthpiece.

NOTES

Index of Saxophone Parts

This is a repeat from the section on pages 2–4, with page numbers for easy reference.

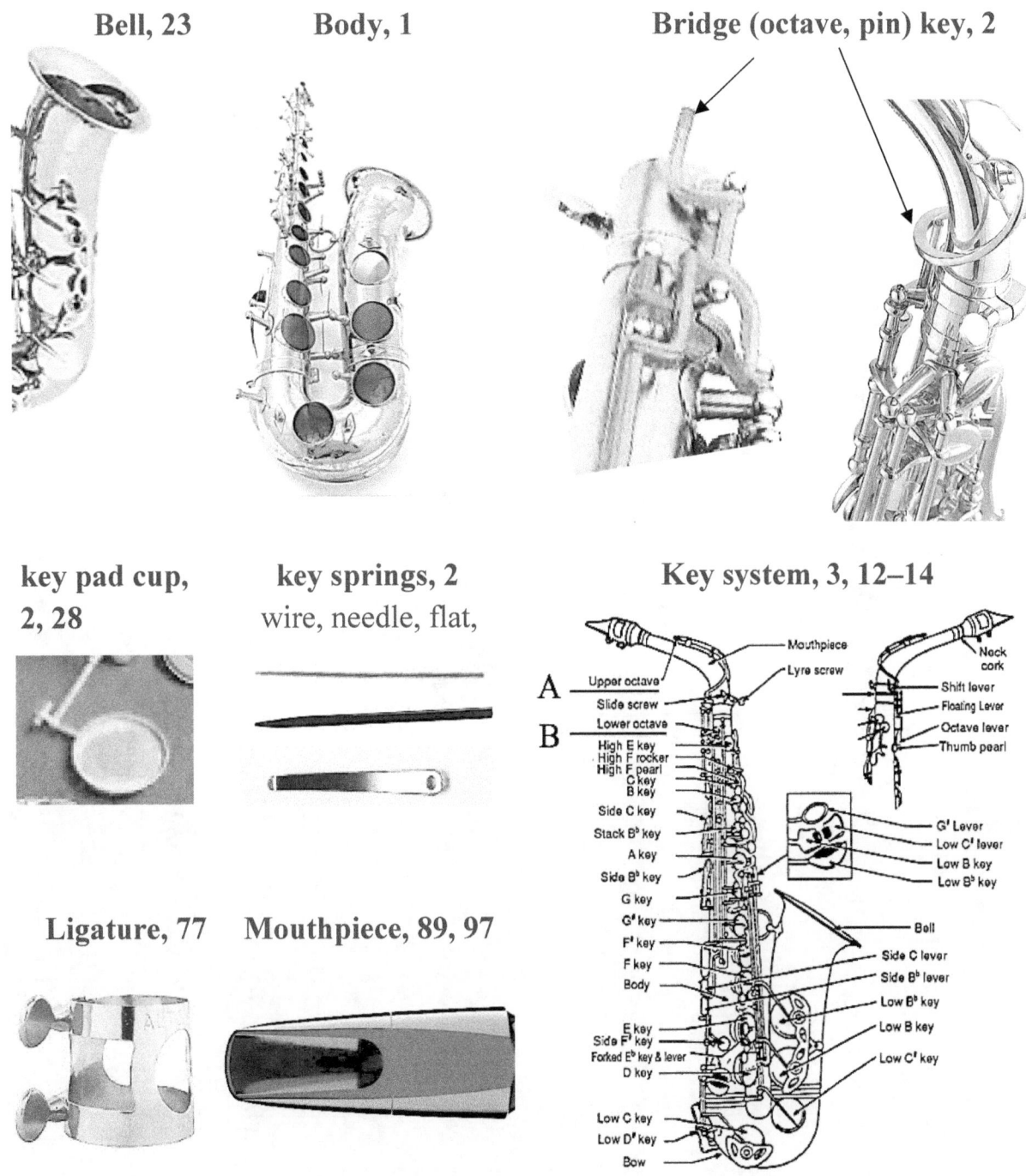

Bell, 23

Body, 1

Bridge (octave, pin) key, 2

key pad cup, 2, 28

key springs, 2
wire, needle, flat,

Key system, 3, 12–14

Ligature, 77

Mouthpiece, 89, 97

Neck, 1–2

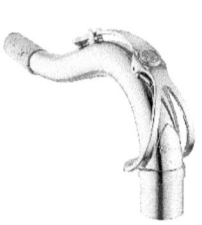

Octave Key, 2

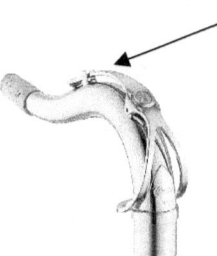

Pad, 2–3

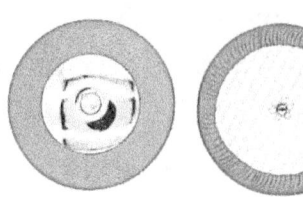

Post, 4, 26

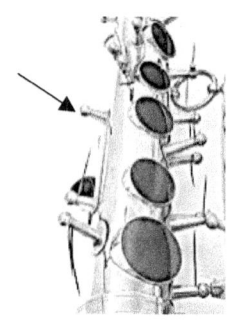

Reed, 74–75

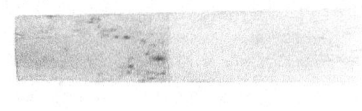

Tenon, 91, 95

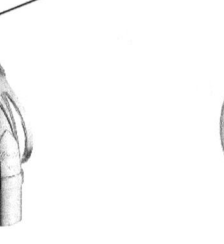

Tone hole, 9

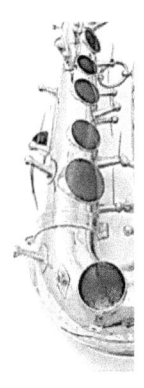

Resonator, 90, 94

Saxophone Mouthpiece Design

At this writing, saxophone mouthpiece design has advanced to the point where there is a design to satisfy almost all possible players' needs. As an introduction to this topic, the following is a summary of information taken with the permission of the website's author: https://theowanne.com/knowledge/baffle-shapes/Theo. This site offers an extraordinary commentary on the various parts of a saxophone mouthpiece and how each affects the sound it produces.

The Chamber

The chamber is the open area in the middle of the mouthpiece under the table.

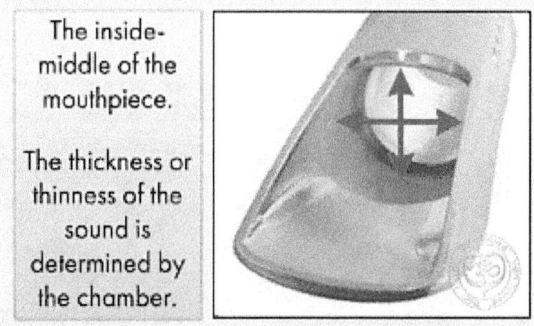

The chamber creates the sound's richness or timbre (see appendix). There are three general types of chambers. These are the large, medium, and small chambers. Each is designed to direct the air stream through the mouthpiece differently.

In a large chamber mouthpiece, the chamber (letter C) is larger than the bore (letter B). This allows the air stream to expand as it moves through the mouthpiece before entering the bore and into the saxophone's neck. The result is a resonant, expansive sound.

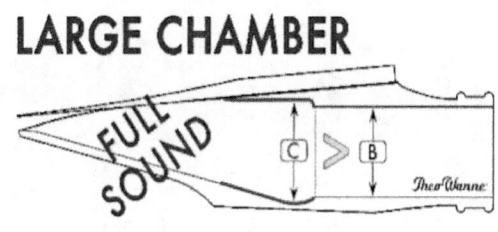

A medium chamber is the same size as the bore (C & B), allowing the air stream to flow uninterrupted through the mouthpiece into the bore. This produces what might be considered to be a fundamental basic saxophone sound.

A small chamber mouthpiece has a chamber that is smaller than the bore (C&B) Constricting the airflow as it travels to the bore. The result is a strong, assertive sound.

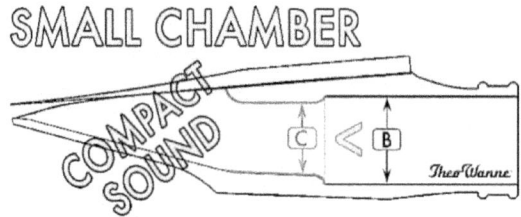

The Baffle

The part of the mouthpiece that creates the biggest difference is the baffle, the section of the mouthpiece directly behind the tip rail that extends back into the mouthpiece about two centimeters. Since the baffle is the first thing the sound wave hits, it has the largest impact on one's sound.

Three kinds of baffles are the flat, rollover, and step baffles.

In the flat baffle design, the airstream travels through the mouthpiece slowly, creating a dark, soft sound with little projection.

The short round tip on the rollover baffle allows most of the air to pass slowly but with a small amount passing more quickly. This creates a darker sound with additional overtones (see appendix) to add an edge to the sound.

The step baffle allows the air to pass through easily without restrictions, resulting in a bright sound.

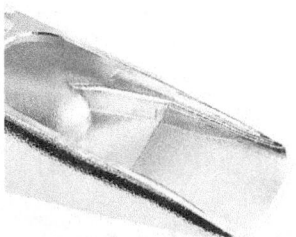

Use this information as a first step to understand the different designs and what each does to your sound production. Trial and error will lead you to the mouthpiece that best suits your sound production goal.

Instrument Ownership Record

This section is designed to document the history and maintenance of an instrument. By entering all the relevant information regularly, you will have a reference for periodic maintenance, information for a possible sale in the future, and a history of the instrument. Not every category listed will be relevant to every instrument. Fill in relevant information and add any information that suits your situation.

(Instrument) _____

Instrument's History

Owner's name _____

Date of purchase _____

Where purchased _____

Brand _____

Model and number _____

Date made _____

New [] previously owned []

Previous owner(s) name(s) _____

Identifying marks, labels, serial number _____

Seller's Information

Name_____

Address_____

Phone_____

Email_____

Website_____

List or asking price_____

Price paid_____

Maintenance Record

When making an entry, include the date, action, repair, replacement or service, part serviced, brand or description of replacement part, source, technician's name, and contact information. Keep all invoices in a file for future reference.

General Service

DATE	SERVICE	TECHNICIAN	COST

Major Repairs

Detail the date, damage, cause, how repaired, by whom, and cost.

DATE	DESCRIBE REPAIR	COST	TECHNICIAN

Index

aulos, 47, 87
Baroque, 45, 57–58, 61, 87, 93
barrel, 87
bass joint, 87
bassoon (history), 59–63
bell, 2, 23–25, 87, 94, 97
billet, 87
bore, 5, 31–33, 46, 48, 52, 55–56, 58–62, 90–91, 93, 99–100
care, 31–38
cases, 76, 79
chalumeau, 48–50, 61, 87
clarineo, 87
clarinet (history) 49–52
Classical, 17, 19, 46, 49 55, 58, 87
closed hole, 87, 89
conservatory system, 59, 87
cork pads, 88
crumhorn, 48–49, 88
dulcian, 59–60
ebonite, 88
facing, 6, 8, 67, 75–76, 88–89, 93–94
fingering, 11–15, 18, 52–53, 62, 88, 93
fipple, 45
fish skin, 9, 88–89, 93–94
flute (history), 46–50
Grenadilla, 92
harmonics, 83–85, 88, 93
Hotteterre, 44, 57, 61
key pad cup, 28, 89, 94, 97
key springs, 2, 36, 89, 94, 97

key system, 3, 9, 11–14, 22, 26–27, 29, 35, 52–53, 57–58, 61–62, 77, 87, 89, 94, 97
kinder Klari, 89
lay, 75, 89, 94
leather pads, 9, 28, 51, 89, 94
ligature, 3, 5–6, 18, 31, 51, 77, 94, 97
lower joint, 21, 89
made (saxophone), 23–28
mouthpiece, 5–10, 31, 54–56, 66–68, 75–77, 87–91, 93–95, 99–101
oboe (history), 57–59
oil, 33-37, 65–66
ophicleide, 29, 53
pad, 3, 9, 28–29, 36–38, 51–53, 88–90, 93–95, 97–98
paddle, 88–89, 94
pitch, 7–8, 20–21, 44, 48–49, 51, 59, 68–70, 81, 83–85, 88–91, 93-95
Plateau Keys, 59, 89
posts, 4, 26, 29, 34–35, 89–90, 94–95
reed, 1, 3, 5-8, 49–52, 74–76, 88–91, 93–96
rib, 26, 90, 94
saxophone (history), 53–56
shawm, 56–57, 59, 90
side rails, 90, 95
silicon, 90, 95
sonic welding, 61, 200
sound production, 5, 90, 95, 101
spatula, 18, 177, 200

spring, 2, 4, 33, 36–37, 88, 90, 93–95, 97
staple, 91
step-up, 91, 95
student-level, 91, 95
tenon, 3, 91, 95, 98
throat, 55–56, 91, 95
tip rail, 91, 95, 100
tone holes, 9–11, 26, 43–45, 47, 49–53, 56, 60–61, 94–95
transposition, 16, 160, 200
tuning, 7, 68–70, 91, 95
upper joint, 91
windcap, 48–49, 56–57, 88, 91
window, 55, 91, 95
wing joint, 91
zummara, 48, 91

www.ingramcontent.com/pod-product-compliance
Lightning Source LLC
Chambersburg PA
CBHW081204240426
43669CB00039B/2804